The Insider's Guide to High School

A Parent's Handbook for the Ninth Grade Year

The Insider's Guide to High School

A Parent's Handbook for the Ninth Grade Year

Tim Healey and Alex Carter

VANDAMERE
PRESS

St. Petersburg, Florida

Published by
Vandamere Press
P.O. Box 149
St. Petersburg, FL 33731
USA

ISBN: 978-0-918339-73-7

To our children:
Anna and Reid Carter, and
Matthew, Elizabeth, and Andrew Healey.
May our advice work as well for you as it does for others.

Table of Contents

Appendices

Acknowledgements

The completion of this book is a dream come true for us. What started as a simple discussion about how we could help parents support their rising ninth-graders' transition to high school turned into a book only because of the support and encouragement so many important and valuable people gave us. These incredible supporters have listened to our discussions, put up with our debates, and have contributed so many ideas that we are forever in their debt.

The first of these stalwart supporters is Sandra Carter, who thought she had earned some time to relax after 40 years in education. Little did she know that she would spend countless hours in her first year of retirement reading and rereading different versions of this book! Her insights into all aspects of this project were invaluable.

We both have had the great pleasure of working closely with Karyn Riddle, without whose loyalty, dedication, and friendship we would be lost. Karyn has patiently listened to our ideas for years. Neither of us has ever met an educator with more common sense or greater ability to "get things done."

Several fantastic parents helped revise our book, including Lindsey Walker, Rick Silverman, and Paula Polglase. Their contributions made this book so much better. Moreover, many people have provided us great insight and support in this endeavor, namely Judy Stockhouse, Phillip Bigler, and Wade Whitehead.

A special thanks to Ron and Gray Bryan, who graciously allowed us to use their vacation home on Hilton Head Island, South Carolina, as a writer's enclave. It was wonderful to get such a huge chunk of the book written in such a beautiful setting. In fact, without this opportunity, we're not sure this project would have ever been completed.

We model ourselves on the great educators with whom we have been honored to work in our careers. Among these influential educators are Wayne Mallard, Kris Pedersen, Walter Bailey, and Cheryl Clements, just to name a few. Many of these wonderful people didn't even know we were writing this book, but they will find that their beliefs and ideas are woven throughout.

We were inspired to write this book by two different sources: our own parents, who nurtured our personal development (which required great patience!) and those parents who make a difference in our schools and with their own children. These parents, who seem like "insiders" themselves, include Rena Stauffer, Mike Holupka, Mike Flynn, and many, many more. These great people became exemplars of those who exhibit the parenting skills we hope to see in schools everywhere.

We both feel very fortunate to work at incredible high schools and in innovative school districts. Our teachers and staff reflect everything that's good in high school education.

We would like to point out the tremendous encouragement of family members, namely Ed Healey, Jr., Ross Carter, Leesa Carter, and David Carter. Most important to the success of this endeavor were Alex's wife, Wendy, and Tim's wife, Nickie, who have endured our hours away from home, not only because of our demanding jobs as high school principals, but also because of the extra time it has taken us to write this book. It short, our families have been amazing. Their support has been our inspiration and their understanding means more to us than they fully realize.

Finally, we deeply appreciate the vision and support of our editor, Pat Berger; our designer, Victor Weaver; and our publisher, Art Brown, at Vandamere Press. Having been in on this project from the earliest conceptual stages, Art's encouragement and guidance have been unwavering. For that, we are eternally grateful.

Foreword

There are no secrets to success. It is the result of preparation, hard work, learning from failure. —Colin Powell

Our motivation for writing this book is clear: We want to see every student succeed in ninth grade. As educators with almost 40 years of combined experience working in high schools with teenage students, we have seen too many great kids struggle and suffer because the guidance they needed was not provided to them. We have also seen too many hard-working parents struggle and suffer along with these ninth graders. We asked ourselves if there was anything we could do to help families get through this difficult and trying, yet exciting and fascinating, time of the high school journey. That was when we decided that this book needed to be written.

The importance of the ninth grade year cannot be overstated. Many consider this year to be the watershed year, the "make-it-or-break-it" year, of students' educational careers. Research shows that, if students fail to succeed during this year, they are much more likely to drop out of high school. Conversely, when students thrive during their freshman year, they are apt to continue to experience great success, not only in high school, but in college and in life. With so much riding on the delicate and important transition to high school, conscientious parents do whatever it takes to support their children during this critical period.

While there are many keys to success, and there is no substitute for hard work, years of experience in the field of education have led us to certain conclusions about the ninth grade year. We know that the ninth grade year is a critical juncture in a child's academic and social development. We also know that this is a time when parents must manage their children skillfully and delicately. We have seen how a student's success or failure during this crucial year can have major implications for both the parents and teen. We realize that involved parents will go to great lengths to help their child. These parents are always looking for advice and insight into ways they can better fulfill their parental role. Even the best of parents, who do all the right things, have children who make mistakes. There is no magic formula for the teenage years and no prescription to follow that ensures success. We believe that parents deserve the type of insider knowledge we provide throughout this book. Our aim is to provide parents with the information that will help them guide their teens to success during the freshman year. We want to give you an advantage when dealing with issues that are likely to arise with respect to your child's school, teachers, and administrators.

We have struggled when deciding to include several of the items and insider's tips in this book. Some strategies that we describe are techniques that we, as school leaders, are reluctant to talk about. To be honest, when we are in our roles as principals, we are not always thrilled when parents use these techniques and strategies. We must admit, however, that these techniques do indeed work for parents and students alike. In our role as "author/consultants," however, we decided to include a description of every technique available to the parent to give them an edge when dealing with the school. We will also try to let you know when a strategy we describe may have unintended consequences. In the end, we wanted to give you, the parent, all of the tools you might need to help your child succeed.

We accept the fact that some in the education community may criticize us for giving parents too much advice and insight. They may say that this is not information parents need, or even should have been given. We believe, however, that you, the parents, are in the best position to know what your children need. Why shouldn't you know everything educators know about *how the system works* or *how the game is played?* Really, every educator's goal is for each student to reach his potential. Therefore, we simply have provided you, as parents, some help to have your teen transition to high school successfully and start them on a positive track for reaching their potential.

Our sincere hope is that after reading this book you will be better equipped with the information and insight that you did not know, and that this knowledge will help you support your teen toward high school success. Some aspects of the book will contain material you may already know. We recognize this and hope that the book validates your beliefs and instincts.

The teenage years can be the most trying times for a parent. Remember that you are not the only parents dealing with these difficult issues. Behind the front doors of houses all across America, parents are struggling to determine the best ways to support their teenagers so that they can be successful in high school and life. This struggle has been going on for generations.

Before you know it, however, these years will be over. Your child will have become a young adult and finished the high school journey. Graduation day is a special day for several reasons, and it is always our favorite day of the year. It is inspiring to watch parents become overcome with pride and joy as their "baby" walks across the stage and receives the diploma that represents all the hard work it has taken to achieve this milestone. During this time, parents and families reflect on the last 18 years of a child's life. Many focus on that first day of kindergarten and all the ups and downs in between, all the struggles and all the joys culminating in one tangible ceremony of an awarding of a high school diploma. It is an emotional day. We tell our graduates that high school graduation will not be the most important day of their entire lives, nor will it be their biggest achievement, but graduation day is the most special day of their life *so far*. Graduation day is a milestone that recognizes that each and every student has overcome obstacles and achieved something special. Many educators think that graduation day is actually for the parents' celebration rather than the students'.

THE ORGANIZATION OF THIS BOOK

We are writing primarily for parents rather than for educators. We have attempted to make this book highly readable, anecdotal, and devoid of the jargon so often used in books about education. It should serve both as a primer to prepare you for your teen's high school experience, and also as a reference that you may need in times of concern or trouble. The first seven chapters provide some proactive steps you can follow to help you and your teen avoid some of the common pitfalls and mistakes that can plague the freshman year. Also, we will provide some resources to fall back on should you have to handle the tough situations that you may, like it or not, be forced to face in the coming years.

Chapter One provides the program goals and an introduction to the concept of success in the freshman year. A second section of that chapter reflects upon your years as a parent and identifies the changing role you have assumed as your child has grown.

Chapter Two, "Make a Plan," explains why it is important for parents to sit with their teen to articulate where they want to be at the end of their high school career. We provide a "vision inventory" that you can complete together and highlight some of the resources you can access as you complete this task.

Chapter Three, "Get Organized," provides an overview of how our best students stay on top of their school work while managing to lead well-balanced and happy high school lives. Too many parents take action *only after their child has started to fall behind academically,* but then it is a much more challenging problem to overcome. As high school insiders, we will tell you how to establish academic protocols and procedures so your student will understand your expectations and will be in the best possible position to succeed.

Chapter Four, "Get Involved," explains the importance of students, as well as parents, in committing to the high school experience by fully engaging in all aspects of school life. Put yourself forward as a role model by demonstrating through your participation that your teen's educational success and happiness are important to you.

Chapter Five, "Form Positive School Relationships," is designed to give you the inside information on how you can work to form positive relationships with the school staff to form a team who will work toward the success of your child. Positive relationships with these key players will "grease the wheels" for your teen's transition to high school.

In Chapter Six, "Every Kid Needs Supervision," you will learn that freshmen are not "all grown up" now. As *high school insiders,* we have seen many students make really poor decisions and get into unnecessary trouble. Many of these students had parents who assumed the job was done and stopped keeping a "close watch" on their teen once he or she hits the ninth grade. We will give you some suggestions about appropriate boundaries and limits for your ninth grade student.

Chapter Seven, "Monitoring Progress," highlights how savvy parents keep tabs on their student's progress while they make their way through the ninth grade year. These astute parents usually seem to intervene before a minor problem becomes a major one. We will provide you with a list of the tools that are likely to be available to you to monitor the progress of your student, so you don't leave your child's success up to chance.

Starting with Chapter Eight, "My Kid's Grades Stink!" our goal is to provide a reference to help guide you through the "hard times." Even if you do everything right, you may find yourself dealing with one of these troubling and serious scenarios. In this section, we give you the insider's edge: the knowledge and foresight you will need to manage your way through these issues with the least possible friction and negative impact on your teen. The most common issue facing freshman parents is discovering that their child's grades aren't up to family expectations.

In Chapter Nine, "My Kid's Teacher Stinks!" we help you understand one of the most difficult problems in parent/educator relationships. There is a good chance that you might have to face this issue at least once during your teen's high school experience. Over the course of your teen's high school career, which will most likely involve 28 different teachers, one of them is likely to be a real stinker! Chapter Nine will help you figure out what to do when your teen is at odds with a teacher. As high school insiders, we give you the best advice on what to consider as you deliberate on this issue. Should you decide to request that your child's schedule be changed, we provide you with procedures and "back door" techniques that will most likely result in your child being placed into a new class quickly.

Chapter Ten, "My Kid's Friends Stink!" explains what you can do as a parent to help your teen make good decisions when selecting friends, and what to do when your child becomes friendly with the "wrong" or "bad" kids. Ninth grade is the time when kids begin to expand their social networks. You may see your teen hanging around with a new and different set of friends during this important transition period. Every parent's nightmare is that their child will begin to "run with a bad crowd." In most cases, your teen's new friends will be pleasant, positive, and normal parts of your child's high school life. In some cases, however, you might suspect that nothing good will come of the associations between your child and some of these new friends. We'll tell you what to do if that becomes the case.

Chapter Eleven, "Oh No! It's the Principal!" has been created to deal with the dreaded phone call from the principal's office. Unfortunately, some students make choices that force their school to take disciplinary actions. As a parent, this puts you in a challenging situation. On the one hand, you want to support your school administration and reinforce the behavior expectations that both you and the principal have for your teen. On the other hand, you want to support your child and make sure that the consequence the school assigns is appropriate and is not going to have a long-lasting impact on any future goals and plans. This is where we give you the insight and support you need to make the best decisions for your teen. We advise you when to support the school and when to "go to bat" for your kid. We give you the insider's information on how best to support your child when you feel that there has been an inappropriate consequence for misbehavior.

Chapter Twelve, "A Brief Look Forward," previews the sophomore year and provides a summary of our main points before we deliver our final thoughts on the freshman year and the high school experience.

Finally, we hope you will find our book to be an easy, down-to-earth read. We purposely designed it to be something any parent could pick up, read quickly, and get some help on the immediate steps to take to support their teen. We wish you the best of luck with your teen's transition to high school and with the next four years. We believe in kids and education. Most importantly, we believe in parents and families supporting their child: Never give up, no matter the how hard the struggle.

Enjoy your successes.

Chapter One

This May Be the Most Important Parenting Book You Will Ever Read

Students' experiences in their first year of high school often determine their success throughout high school and beyond. However, more students fail ninth grade than any other grade. —Williams & Richman, 2007

As the parent of a rising ninth grade student, you are about to embark upon a journey that has become so perilous that it is currently the focus of dozens of research studies all around the United States. Too many students fail their freshman year! The importance of the ninth grade year is paramount. According to researchers, students' success in high school, as well as in their post-secondary future, is significantly impacted by what happens during the ninth grade year. Studies suggest that 33% of the students who completed eighth grade last year will not graduate from high school four years from now, and more students fail ninth grade than any other grade. A student who does not successfully complete the necessary credits needed for promotion to tenth grade is *twenty times* more likely to drop out of high school. These data are extremely disturbing and troubling. Schools across the nation take this problem very seriously. And so do we.

In addition to the purely educational issues, sociologists have long identified the ages fourteen- and fifteen-years (the typical ages for those students entering ninth grade) to be a defining period for teenagers. During this time your teen is likely to have problems adjusting to new situations. Teens have been shown to have increased anxiety and social difficulty, decreased feelings of connectedness, and, changes in their relationships with their parents.

Doesn't this sound like the perfect time to throw your kid into a new school situation, one with added responsibility and pressure? Your teen is about to become a member of the newest class of high school freshmen. We're guessing that you are feeling a little bit overwhelmed. Don't be. We are here to help! By following our suggestions and tips, we will prepare you to be a savvy parent throughout your teen's transition to high school.

We have given the advice contained within this book so many times during conferences with parents or disciplinary hearings, *after* mistakes have been made. We wrote this book so we could be proactive, sharing tips with parents, *before* their children begin to struggle. We want parents to have access to our knowledge, our high school insiders' knowledge, that will provide the support, information, and understandings that will make their jobs as parents much easier and more enjoyable.

We hope that this book arms you with the knowledge and insider's understandings that will help you guide your freshman to a successful future. We know that you can use the information we have provided to avoid some of the common pitfalls and dangers of this very important year.

REFLECTIONS ON GOOD PARENTING

Since you are reading this book, we know that you are a committed and dedicated parent who does whatever it takes to find the answers you need to provide the best support possible for your child. As we prepare to guide you through the next stage of your parental role, it would be beneficial to reflect upon the past to review what has happened so far and provide you with a broad overview of what may likely occur over the next four years.

This scenario may sound familiar:

> *As my daughter got off the bus after completing her last day of eighth grade, it hit me. Next year she would be going to high school. As each day of summer passed, I grew more and more anxious. I knew that soon I would be sending my child to face*

the trials of high school. When she was smaller, I remember driving by the high school and being terrified that some day I would send my baby to such a huge and scary looking school. It looked so big, more like an uninviting government building than the small, friendly school I had been used to! Now when we drive by the high school, my daughter too seems completely overwhelmed. How will she find her way around? Will she know which class is meeting next? Can she handle the rigors of high school courses? Will she be pushed around by the older, bigger, and maybe rougher kids? I have even heard horrible stories from my friends and neighbors about what a challenge it is to work with the high school administrators; how mean the teachers are; how impersonally everyone is treated. And worst of all, the only thing I remember from high school is the time Mr. Jones pointed out that I was drooling on the desk as I slept through his U.S. History class. I don't want my teen to be humiliated! I remember thinking at my high school graduation, "Thank goodness I will never have to live through this again." Yet, here I am. What's worse is that now I am the parent—the one who is supposed to have all the answers!

As you have progressed as a parent, you have adapted to the changing demands and needs of your child. In each stage of your child's life you have learned new skills and techniques necessary for you to perform the functions of a "good" parent. While we don't claim to be experts on all these stages, our experience as educators and parents lead us to believe that our basic and simple descriptions of these stages are on target.

Prenatal Through Infant

You were the total caregiver to this helpless and innocent living being. From the moment you found out that a baby was on the way, you changed how you lived to provide the best environment for your child's successful development. From finding the best doctor, to taking prenatal vitamins, to eliminating alcohol and tobacco, even to playing your unborn child classical music *in utero* (!), there was no limit to what you would be willing to do to support your child who was totally dependent on your care for survival.

Toddler Through Preschool

As your child grew, you learned to allow some space, but not too much! While your toddler began to make friends and experience playtime, you provided direct supervision. You were still in total control of every decision (choosing outfits and food), but you enjoyed watching your child develop as an individual. You enjoyed the complete trust of your toddler. Like any good parent, you provided structure, consistency, and love, read books nightly, limited exposure to television, and you ensured that your child had the best opportunities to gain the experiences necessary to grow into a happy, healthy youngster.

Elementary School

We all remember our child's first day of kindergarten. Were you the parent who put your child on the bus and then sped to school to watch them get off the bus and walk into school? You wanted to hear every detail about what went on in school that day, and your kindergartener was only too happy to share it with you. As the years went on, you became more comfortable with your child being away from you for many hours, but you were still well aware and informed about how class time was spent each day. Do you remember how nurturing and friendly the school was, how much the school appreciated and wanted parent volunteers, and how easily you related to your child's teachers? These were the easy years.

Middle School

As your child entered middle school, you began to see a more independent and headstrong individual develop; yet, you still felt in control. You knew most of the children that your child socialized with and, most likely, you knew their parents as well. The role you played at school had also changed, but you felt that you understood the subjects and felt a part of the "team" that was educating your child.

High School: "In Like a Lion; Out Like a Lamb"

We compare the role you will play as a parent to your high school student to the old adage about the month of March, "In like a lion, out like a lamb." Just as the month of March changes dramatically from the cold, hard days of winter to the warm and pleasant days of spring, your teen will change dramatically from the summer after the eighth grade year until graduation. Just as the child is changing, successful parents change their methods and tactics as well. You need to start off the high school years like a lion.

The Ninth Grade Year

Without a doubt, the ninth grade year is the most important and crucial year for high school success. We like to think of ninth-graders as "big middle schoolers." In general, freshmen are still rather immature, awkward, and naïve about the ins and outs of what it takes to be successful in high school. We tend to see a great deal of "drama," some lingering bullying, and a lack of vision for the future. In short, it is a very complex developmental year in a child's life. Our "Six Steps" will help you assist your teen to make it rather than break it during this crucial developmental period. We recommend that parents proactively keep a close watch on their teen's progress, actively monitoring all aspects of their child's life. We will define what is appropriate monitoring for the ninth grade year in the following chapters; but generally this is where you will act like the "lion," protecting your teen from making decisions that will negatively impact their future.

The Rest of High School

The role you play as a ninth grade parent is likely to have a huge impact on the amount of work you'll need to do during the next three years. If your high schooler has a successful ninth grade year, the odds are that you will see these skills and habits continue to foster success throughout your teen's high school career. Those tenth graders who were successful in ninth grade are usually on track for success and matriculate to their eleventh grade year in good standing. The junior year is often the most stressful and academically challenging year of high school (*and will be the focus of our next book*). Fortunately for parents, eleventh graders tend to have developed a greater focus and vision for their future and are more willing to accept the help and guidance from the adults in their lives. This is where you will act more like the quiet "lamb," assisting your teen to make good decisions in a quiet and unobtrusive way, showing that you have confidence that your teenager has become competent at making good decisions. During the senior or twelfth grade year, you will start to see that your student has begun to form his self-image as an adult.

So now that you are getting ready to be the parent of a high school student, your role will begin to evolve. It's most important to know that for the first time in your child's academic life the decisions and performances of your ninth grader will have a *real* and *significant* impact on his or her future. During these four years, your role will be part advisor, evaluator, motivator, and cheerleader. You will have to know when to put on pressure and when to take the pressure off. More importantly, parents have to judge when to stand up for their children, when to support the administration, and when to let their child handle problems on their own.

Chapter Two

Make a Plan

If you don't know where you're going, the chances are you'll end up somewhere else.   —Yogi Berra

Imagine getting into your car on a beautiful sunny day, starting the engine, putting the car in gear, and driving away from your home. You have no destination in mind. How might this affect your trip? Chances are you won't be driving very fast because you will be in no particular hurry to get anywhere. If you happen to encounter obstacles along the way (construction delays, traffic, etc.), you will most likely give up on your current path and choose another, easier, less challenging route. You will probably have very low expectations for your trip, and if you do encounter any positive outcomes, you will attribute it to "dumb luck."

Although this aimless, totally spontaneous sounding excursion might sound like a fun exercise for a day trip on a free and sunny day, it would be a poor and largely unproductive way to undertake a serious, life-altering journey. The average person wouldn't think of wasting a three-day weekend traveling so aimlessly, let alone undertake a monumentally important expedition without a clear plan for success. We all know that, even with a clear vision of where you are going and with a logical plan on how to get there, trips don't always go as expected!

When Christopher Columbus left Spain in 1492, he knew exactly where he was going. He had a rough map of the world that he was confident would help him navigate the great Atlantic Ocean. According to his calculations, he would make landfall approximately 2,500 miles west of Spain somewhere in Asia. We all know that his trip, despite his careful preparation and dutiful execution, didn't go as planned. His map was incomplete, and while he thought he had reached Asia, he had really found the New World. Yet, even as Columbus failed to achieve his goal in opening a westward route to Asia, his careful planning and preparation enabled him to experience success.

> *When she finished eighth grade, Sara had no idea what she wanted to be when she grew up. She liked school and excelled in all of her subjects, but felt no particular "calling" to one profession or another. Was it a miracle that this seemingly aimless student ended up a National Merit Scholar in the top 1% of her graduating class, and was accepted into an elite university? Not really. Sara had a clear and articulated plan and the support of her parents. This set her up for success in high school.*

Remarkably, we have found that the average student entering ninth grade has done little more planning than our driver did before the imaginary trip we described at the beginning of this chapter. When we ask the question, "Which classes are you taking your freshman year," a ninth grade student can usually answer without any problem. However, when we ask the question, "Why are you taking these classes?," the response is usually a confused, "Huh?"

It is surprising how little the average student thinks about his or her chosen academic path as they enter the four most critical years of their schooling. This lack of vision, planning, and preparation sets countless freshmen down a path toward failure. Like our aimless traveler, a freshman who doesn't have a clear vision and plan tends to move through school without any sense of urgency. Successful students attack their classes with vigor and focus. When obstacles present themselves, aimless students are quick to abandon their path and go in another, less challenging direction. Successful students, on the other hand, strive to overcome obstacles and remain determined to succeed despite any challenge they may face. Our best students have a clear vision for their future and a well-conceived plan to get them there. These goals encourage them to stay committed and focused on success in school.

In an effort to help students avoid the common pitfalls many freshmen have suffered, we have developed some steps you should complete with your freshmen as soon as possible. These steps will help you and your teen form a clear vision of *where you are going, and how you will reach this goal.*

> *Chris is an athletic, outgoing, and fun-loving student who thanks his parents for his success in high school. He says that he had the vague notion as a rising freshman that he might want to be a teacher, but the idea was fuzzy at best. He did know, however, that he would want to attend a top-tier university after high school, and to do that, he knew that he needed to earn good grades in his classes and prepare to score high on his college boards. When asked if he had a great deal of input choosing his freshman courses, he replied, "Heck no! My parents did all the choosing for me. They talked with my guidance counselor, and together decided which courses would put me on the right path to earn the attention of the best universities." As he progressed through high school, he was given more control in choosing his courses. The grades he earned were the result of a lot of hard work on his part, but he gives all the credit for getting off on the right foot during his freshman year to his parents, who were involved in every step of developing his plan.*

VISUALIZE YOUR DESTINATION

Sometimes simple quotes contain the most wisdom. To paraphrase Yogi Berra, unless you have a clear vision of where you are going, you never really know where you are going to end up. The first step for any teen to get on the road to high school success is to determine where they want to go after graduation. For Chris, there was never a question of what he would be doing after high school. Just like most of our top students, he had always known that he would go to college, and his parents never entertained the notion that this wouldn't be the case. Taking this general understanding and honing it into a clear, defined vision, however, was an important step in realizing his dreams of attending a great university.

Sometimes we work with parents to help them understand that it doesn't matter where the parents want their child to be. It is the student who must have a clear vision of their future, and then it is the student who must commit to doing what it takes to reach that goal.

We know that rising freshmen often have wild and unrealistic dreams for their futures. If we had a quarter for every time we've met a future pop idol, professional athlete, or movie star, we'd be very wealthy men. Unfortunately, an incredibly small percentage of these dreams ever come true, but it is good for young people to have these dreams. In fact, we worry about those kids who don't dream big. It is important, however, to begin to develop a back-up plan now, as they are entering the high school years. We want students to begin to be realistic about their futures without crushing their dreams.

We have developed the Insider's Edge Vision Inventory shown in Table 1 to help you begin a discussion with your student. Most successful people understand that the physical act of writing down one's goals is a powerful and important step toward achieving them. In this exercise, we want both you and your child to take the time to complete this vision inventory. It is important for you to accept and validate your teen's hopes and dreams for the future. Encourage your ninth grade student to "reach for the stars." Write down what needs to be done and what needs to happen for these dreams to be realized. While we want students to embrace these dreams, we also want them to develop an appreciation for the hard work, talent, luck, and other intangible factors that it will take for these dreams to come true. If you would like to see a sample completed vision inventory, we have included one in Appendix A.

Table 1. Insider's Edge Vision Inventory

Parent(s)	Rising Ninth Grade Student
What are your dreams for the future for your teen? (Reach for the stars!)	What are your dreams for the future? (Reach for the stars!)
What will it take for your teen to achieve these dreams?	What will it take for you to achieve these dreams?
What is a great "back-up plan" for your teen?	What is your "back-up plan" for your future?
What will it take for your teen to achieve this "back-up plan"?	What will it take to achieve this "back-up plan"?

Matty Symons

Without a clear, articulated vision of where you are going, high school is an easy place to get lost in the crowd.

After you have adopted a realistic view of the future dreams, you will want to encourage your teen to visualize a great "back-up plan." For many rising ninth graders, this is harder than it sounds. They have no idea what they want to do as an adult for a "real" job. That's okay! Next, have your teen describe how they would like their life to be. Where do they want to be living? Describe a dream house and the kind of car they want to drive. This information will give you the data you will need to assess the type of salary your child would have to earn to comfortably live this type of lifestyle. Now you will have a good idea of the type of education/training your child will need to attain that standard of living.

We think it is important that both the parent and the student participate in this exercise. The plan you develop is really only a catalyst to begin the discussion about the path the student must take in order to best prepare and reach the dreams and expectations they have for their future. Remember, the purpose of this exercise is to support your teen's dreams while coaching and assisting to help adopt a realistic and acceptable back-up plan.

DO YOUR HOMEWORK!

Before you can start to outline a plan to help your student get into a position to realize their dreams, you need to know as much about your school system as possible. Every school, school district, and state department of education has different programs for, and requirements of, students. As a parent, you will want to be a well-informed consumer. In order to make the best plan possible for your student, you will want to have a firm grasp of the following information particular to your school/district/state.

What Are Your School's/District's/State's Graduation Requirements?

States and school divisions have different requirements for graduation. States often have multiple diploma types available for graduates. Depending on your student's goals for their future, one type of diploma may be better suited to help them to reach their dreams. Before you help your student determine an academic path, you will want to understand the requirements needed to earn the best diploma for this type of career path.

Are There any Specialty Programs/Special Curricular Opportunities Available to Your Student?

Many school divisions offer specialty programs or special academic opportunities for students with special interests and/or talents. Schools have specialized programs from which students can benefit, such as Advanced Placement courses, the International Baccalaureate Programme, the Cambridge Programme, Centers for Information Technology and/or Computer Science, and certification programs for vocations and trades. Research the schools in your area to find out which school or program is best for your teen. You will want to explore all of these opportunities to weigh the benefits and requirements of each program. Don't let your family's finances get in the way; there are usually scholarships available for students in need. No school worth its salt is going to deprive a student of the opportunities to participate because of a lack of family resources.

What Are the Extra or Co-Curricular Opportunities at Your School?

The research on this is clear: *Students who participate in extra and co-curricular activities are more successful than their peers* who opt not to participate in additional school programs. Active students have higher academic achievement, lower drug and alcohol abuse rates, far lower teen pregnancy rates, and fewer teen suicides. As school insiders, we can tell you through our reflective practice that the students who are most likely to succeed not only in high school, but also in college and in life, are those who become active in one or more extra or co-curricular organizations early in their high school careers. Most schools offer a list of these sports, clubs, and organizations on their web pages. If there isn't such a list, ask your school's Activities Director for this information. (See Chapter 4: "Get Involved!")

NOW MAKE THE PLAN!

Now that you have visualized your student's destination, it is time for you to sit down with your teen and make a plan for how to get there. We know that it is highly likely that this plan is going to change dramatically between now and graduation; but nonetheless, we feel that this is a necessary and useful step in starting high school with a sense of purpose and direction. Getting that "A" in ninth grade History seems a great deal more important if students understands how that "A" is putting them one step closer to their goals and dreams. We have provided you with the Insider's Edge format to develop a Post-Secondary Plan for this planning discussion shown in Table 2. If you would like to see a sample completed Post-Secondary Plan, we have included several in Appendix B.

We feel that it is important that you spend some time with your teen completing this form before the beginning of the fresh-

Table 2. Insider's Edge Post-Secondary Plan

POST-SECONDARY PLAN	
Primary Ambitions	*Realistic "Back-Up" Plan*
State your chosen plan	*State your chosen back-up plan:*
What level of education, training, preparation, and other factors will you need to achieve this goal? *Education:* *Training:* *Preparation:* *Other factors:*	*What level of education, training, preparation, and other factors will you need to achieve this goal?* *Education:* *Training:* *Preparation:* *Other factors:*
Describe what type of high school achievement will likely be necessary for you to realize this ambition:	*Describe what type of high school achievement will likely be necessary for you to realize this ambition:*
What other activities will increase your chances of realizing this goal?	*What other activities will increase your chances of realizing this goal?*

man year. This plan will by no means be complete during this first meeting. You will likely come back to it time and again to amend, alter, or even completely change the plan as time goes by. Nevertheless, we feel that this exercise will put both you and your child on the right track toward high school success.

Chapter Three

Get Organized

The secret of all victory lies in the organization of the non-obvious.
—Emperor Marcus Aurelius

Marcus Aurelius won his victories and became Emperor of the Roman Empire by figuring out how to organize the "non-obvious". We have good news for you: You don't have to be as clever as Marcus was to help your student prepare for success in high school. Success as a ninth-grader is possible simply by organizing the *obvious!* Good planning, clear procedures, and protocols for doing schoolwork at home, a clear understanding of what is expected by the teachers, and excellent time management are the keys to high school academic success. In this chapter, we give you the insider's advice on how to make sure your student is prepared for success in all of these areas.

PROTOCOLS AND PROCEDURES FOR SUCCESS

Parents of our most successful students will tell you that there is definitely a "method to the madness." Their students have developed, often under the direct supervision of their parents, some tried and true protocols and procedures that put them on the path toward high school academic success. Below, we have detailed some of the most effective strategies that our most successful students use for you to consider using with your ninth grader.

Use a Daily Planner

One of the greatest trends in schooling in the last 20 years has been for schools to provide their students with a daily planner used to keep track of day-to-day assignments, appointments, and reminders. This practice has become almost universal. Most of these daily planners are custom-made for the school and include items such as maps, school calendars, student handbooks, and other important information. If your school does not provide a daily planner or day timer to your student, be sure to go out and buy one yourself. This purchase will become one of the best investments of your life!

The life of the average high school student is unbelievably hectic and busy. Even for those of us who were in high school only 25 years ago, it seems that so much more is required of our students today. We wonder how they can fit it all in. What's more amazing is that what we're describing is the norm for the average student. Our top students' lives are so busy that it is truly mind-boggling!

Considering the incredibly busy schedules our students must juggle, we find it surprising (and sometimes disheartening) that so few students use their daily planner on a regular basis. This fact is especially true when considering that it is so evident that those students who do use them benefit greatly from their use.

Students who use their planners regularly tend to fall into two general categories. The first group is made up of those students who are naturally organized and wouldn't consider going through a class, much less an entire school day, without a planner. If your teen is like one of these students, we only have five words of advice for you—get out of the way. This kind of student is a gift, and a rare one! If your child isn't a member of this category, don't worry. It means they are like the other 98% of high school students. You need to be a more pro-active parent to make sure they "see the light!"

The second group is made up of those students who use their daily planners regularly because their parents insist they do. These parents have established some protocols and procedures with their students, and many claim that daily planner use is first and foremost among them. We've discussed these protocols with different parents and they usually have some commonalities, including the following:

- The student will write down the daily assignment for each class in the planner each time the class meets. This practice is important for consistency and serves as a good reference if later the teacher reports missing work.

- The student should write down important due dates for long-term class assignments in the planner as soon as they are announced. The student will write down several "checkpoint" dates in the planner, usually halfway between the day the project was assigned and the due date and another two or three days prior to the due date. This practice helps the student avoid procrastination.

- The student will keep track of important meetings of clubs, sporting events, concerts, activities, and any other activities that require the student's afternoon, evening, or weekend time. This practice is also helpful for the parents, since they will quite often need to coordinate their schedules with these events so they can attend as well. (See Chapter 4—"Get Involved")

- Finally, the daily planner is the place for your student to keep track of personal appointments, friends and study partners' phone numbers and email addresses, birthdays, and social events, etc.

Alex Carter

High school is a very busy and hectic time of life. Students who use their daily planners regularly find it much easier to stay on track and succeed in school.

Many people are using new "smart phones" to take the place of all paper and pencil daily planners. For students this technology can be problematic because of district and school rules that often prohibit students from using electronics during the school day. Should school rules change to fit this new paradigm, "daily planner" should be used as a universal term for any mechanism one can use to keep track of the student's busy schedule.

Savvy parents will establish a clear routine from the beginning of the school year of checking their teen's planner every day. This check is a great way to stay informed about what is going on in your student's life and to stay aware of upcoming assignments and events.

The bottom line is that maintaining the daily planner regularly and completely makes the life of a high school student much more manageable and enjoyable for everyone concerned. It also establishes a lifelong organizational habit that has benefits in college and beyond.

Insider's Tip: Procrastination is the enemy of student success. Using the daily planner and staying on top of homework, test preparation, and class projects are keys to ninth grade success.

Define the Rules for How Work Will Be Done at Home

Something we see time and again is that the parents of our most successful students have created a set of rules and practices that define how schoolwork is done at home. These simple protocols and procedures are developed by both the parents and the students at the beginning of the year and are agreed upon by everyone. These protocols might include the following:

- The student works on homework at the same time every day.
- There is a clean, professional, quiet workspace provided to complete out-of-school assignments.
- All major assignments will be shared and reviewed with the parents.

These simple rules make the routine clear to the student. They show that the parents expect all work to be completed in a timely and organized fashion. They show that the parents respect that this work is going to be difficult at times, and that the student needs a place to work free of distractions such as little brothers or sisters. Also, these rules show that the parent is still an important part of the schooling process.

Parents have asked us whether they should let their student do their homework in their bedrooms. Our advice is simple: "If it works - yes! If it doesn't - no!" What we think is most important is that all parties understand that these rules are adjustable and can become more complex or eased as the freshman progresses. If everything is going great, the child receives more freedom and independence in how and when to complete the work. If things are not so great, the parent may become even more involved. The bottom line is, however, at no point should parents indicate to the student that they are "on their own." Savvy parents are always aware of what is going on and know how and when to show they are aware of the student's progress.

Be Sure That Teacher Expectations Are Understood

One of the hardest things for students to experience is when they spend a great deal of time on a project or assignment, only to find out later that the teacher's expectations were very different from what they had produced. Remarkably, this is a common occurrence in high school. One of the traits of our most successful students is that they never undertake a major project until they are sure they are on the right track. One of the keys to these students' success is that they are usually working on the projects well in advance of the due date. This practice allows them to ask the right questions of the teachers if they need clarification or are confused about the assignment. This situation is a perfect example of why procrastination is the enemy of student success. If students are working on projects at the last minute, they are forced to do what they think (or they hope!) the teacher wants. Students who start early have time to find out what the expectations are so they know they will be successful on the assignment and in the class.

Good Time Management Is Essential to Success in High School

As we said earlier in this chapter, students often have unbelievably busy schedules. On top of a rigorous curriculum, they may have sporting practices and games, club meetings, music concerts, school dances, along with a myriad of other events and obligations that fill up every minute of their days. Additionally, top students often are elected to leadership roles in their various clubs and organizations, so their time is even more consumed with the planning, organization, and running of the various clubs and organizations they lead. It can get overwhelming! Our most successful students, however, manage all the parts of their busy lives and still seem to appear happy, well adjusted, and eager to come back to school for more. How do they do it?

These students succeed by managing their time wisely. They have "all of their ducks in a row" before they engage in any activity. In discussions with these top students over the years, we have learned they are shrewd in the way they handle their responsibilities. We have identified some of the habits students' exhibit. These students have the following characteristics:

- **Always put academics first.** If they feel that they have too much on their plates, they quickly let their sponsors or club advisors know they might need help fulfilling their extracurricular responsibilities. These students aren't afraid to ask for help when they are feeling overwhelmed, but they never leave anything "hanging" without ensuring someone else has picked up the slack.
- **Prioritize their responsibilities on a daily basis.** These students will frequently make "to do" lists, placing the most important items at the top and will work down to the less important items when time permits. They keep careful records of what they have completed and what there is yet to do. These students are methodical in their work.

- **Are acutely aware of upcoming due dates.** They frequently review their schedules to make sure that everything is on track for timely completion. They are sure to look forward in their schedules to predict what is going to put pressure on them in the near future and, when possible, they will try to get ahead.
- **Know when to say when!** Most of these top students have learned the hard way never to bite off more than they can chew. Once they have filled their schedules, they typically will not add anything more to their agenda. If an opportunity that is "too good to be true" comes by, they will find something to eliminate from their schedule before agreeing to take on a new venture or responsibility.

In conclusion, the freshman year is an important transition year for students. They are learning to become more independent and take more responsibilities while discovering their interests and limitations. Throughout this process, they need the help and support from their parents. Parents need to set the boundaries, create the environment in which the student can succeed, and provide their teens the support they need by offering careful advice and words of wisdom and encouragement.

Chapter Four

Get Involved

When we talk with parents of ninth grade students who have had a successful transition to high school, we ask them what made the difference for their teen. Without hesitation, the majority of these parents say, "My child became involved in school activities outside of the classroom that helped make a connection to the school in addition to the normal connections of the regular classroom setting."

INVOLVED STUDENTS AND PARENTS EXPERIENCE MORE SUCCESS

Research shows that students involved in an activity, club, sport, music, etc. (either connected to the school or outside of school), are much more likely to have a positive high school experience and earn better grades than students who are not involved. To take this a step further, as high school insiders, we can assure you that the most successful students are the ones whose parents participate in the school by attending functions, joining the PTO (PTA), and help with the Athletic Boosters, Advisory Councils, chaperoning, or just volunteer around the school. In a sense, these parents are the ones that are "in the know," and they use this information to support their teen and the school.

Does This Sound Like You?

Specifically, we remember a discussion with one parent who said that she was concerned when thinking about her son going to high school. She told us that she would literally lie awake at night thinking about "her child" moving up to high school. She recounted how her stress level increased every time she thought about how big the building was, how many students went there, and how her teen would handle having to adjust to all the changes in his life now that he is in high school. Her son had been really shy in middle school. She appreciated the nurturing culture of the middle school that had guarded him against negative influences. She wondered how he would handle all of this by himself. Will he get lost? Will he make friends? Will he be able to succeed in class?

Now, after two months of high school, she didn't think twice about crediting her son's involvement with marching band as the main reason for his successful transition to high school. She quickly pointed out that it had nothing to do with the quality of the band or the benefits of playing a musical instrument. He transitioned successfully to high school because of the connections he had made with other students *as a result of his involvement with the marching band.* In a sense, he had something that was all his own. He belonged! He had found his place in the high school, and this was accomplished before the first day of the school year! The marching band started practicing during the summer in a band camp. She said that this helped him make friends and become comfortable with the school even before his first day of classes. These connections allowed him to feel confident and secure from the very first day of school. He was not scared at all on the first day of school (although she still was!). At lunch, he sat with some of his friends from marching band. When he got turned around in the building trying to find his classroom, he ran in to a senior band member who helped him find his way. This connection had a hugely positive impact on his overall success transitioning to high school.

The Spill-Over Effect

This student's mom shared how wonderful everything had been the first two months of high school. Her son's classes were going well, his grades were good, and he had made many new friends. Overall, he would arrive home each day talking about how much he loved school,

Jose Gil

Ninth graders are encouraged to get involved in extra-curricular activities such as band early in their high school careers to provide them a quick introduction to high school life.

marching band, and the whole high school experience. Really, she just had positive things to say about high school and her son's transition. There is a common saying among families, "When Momma's happy, everyone's happy." In high schools the saying is more like this: "When the child's happy, then Momma's happy. When Momma's happy, the family is happy. When the family is happy, the principal doesn't get any complaints."

THE NEXT STEP

The late Tim Russert, former host of NBC's *Meet the Press* and author of *Wisdom of Our Fathers,* said as advice to parents, "You can shower a child with presents or money, but what do they really mean, compared to the most valuable gift of all—your time? Vacations and special events are nice, but so often the best moments are the spontaneous one. Being there! Every moment you spend with your child could be the one the really matters."

Of course, the next step in this relationship (as we explained to this mom) is for her to get involved with the other amazing supportive parents in marching band or becoming part of the Principal's Advisory Council. Unequivocally, this would complete her son's transition to high school and help her be the best parent she can be over his next years of high school.

Most people will tell you that there isn't a lot of parental involvement in high schools. We disagree with this statement and would challenge any of these naysayers to observe a typical high school on any Friday night across the country. Parents are everywhere! Parents are helping the band carry instruments; parents are announcing games; parents are working in the concession stands; parents are helping the activities director run events. If you doubt this example, then just attend a high school swim meet. Week in and week out, these meets are entirely run by parents. There are opportunities to become an involved parent in academic areas as well as in volunteer efforts to support groups such as the Model United Nations, Forensics Debate Tournaments, and drama productions.

> *Insider's Tip: Your high school should be able to provide you with a list of all clubs, activities, and sports and with the contact information of the sponsors for each. Ask for this information in the spring of your child's eighth grade year.*

The parents who get involved with the school (at whatever level) usually are more connected, confident, and prepared to handle any issues that may arise in their teen's school life. They know the teachers, administrators, and other parents. They are comfortable meeting the principal in the hallway, at a school concert, or another school event. These parents' children receive a clear message that they are supported and that their parents know what's going on at the school. Really, this is quite powerful.

THE BEST PART

It doesn't matter what the activity is as long as your teen is involved with some *positive activity*. Most high schools have a comprehensive list of sports, clubs, and activities to join. Kids do not have to fit a certain mold to be active in their school. Schools have come a long way from just having a few opportunities for a few students to be involved. There is something fun for everyone!

> *Insider's Tip: If your teen is too shy to go to an activity/club meeting, email the sponsor or guidance counselor and ask if he will speak to and encourage your child to attend the first activity/club gathering.*

DON'T OVEREXTEND YOUR CHILD

The benefit of joining a club or trying out for a team is for your child to enjoy the additional connection to high school. The research is clear in all the other positive effects this involvement provides. However, be careful as a parent not to let your teen overextend with these activities even if many of the opportunities are appealing. The goal is not to simply create a long laundry list of activities to be impressive on college applications. While it is true that colleges and universities want to recruit well-rounded, involved young people, they really prefer students involved in a few, quality activities. They are especially interested in students who have risen to leadership positions in these groups.

As a parent of a rising ninth grader, don't worry about creating a list of activities for your teen. Right now, your first priority is to ease the transition to high school. Help your child find a few activities to enjoy at school, but keep it balanced so that there is still the time for academic studies. In other words, if your teen doesn't have enough time to keep up with homework because of the time it takes to be involved in activities, this simply defeats the purpose. What you want to see are positive connections for your child outside the classroom, but start slowly. Teenagers should be encouraged to take on one new activity at a time and show that they can handle the responsibilities of the classroom first and the fun and enjoyment of the club/activity second.

James Boardman

Student involvement in high school sports has been shown to correlate with healthier choices and better grades, not to mention a happier, more engaged high school experience.

ACTIVITIES OUTSIDE OF SCHOOL ARE GOOD TOO

Activities outside of school are important, too. Some of the most successful high school students are highly involved in Boy/Girl Scouts of America, religious/church youth groups, and other non-school related groups. Studies have certainly shown the positive effects on teenagers for these groups.

These outside groups are highly regarded by most colleges/universities, and your teen should be encouraged to continue being involved with them. While these activities may not directly help with the ninth grade transition, they can help with the overall development and maturity of young people.

"THERE'S NO ACTIVITY FOR MY CHILD"

Many high schools offer a myriad of activities and clubs that attempt to appeal to a wide range of student interests. Still, some parents get frustrated because they feel that there is not an activity or club that connects to their teen's interests. If you find yourself struggling with your teen at finding the right activity or club, consider some of the following ideas.

Look at this problem as an opportunity to begin a discussion with your teen about the fact that, as they get older, their interests will change. Part of growing up is trying different activities to see if they are appealing or worthwhile. Remind them that no matter the outcome of their efforts at trying a new club, they will meet new people, have new are interesting experiences, and, possibly, even make additional friends.

Some of the clubs associated with a high school will be service-oriented. These clubs offer a prime opportunity to discuss the merits of giving back to the community and providing volunteer work for those less fortunate. Often times, the service-oriented clubs, the Key Club for instance, will not appeal to a ninth grader because they really don't understand what the name of the club means. Upon discovering that the Key Club (or another similar club) provides valuable community service may change their initial reaction to the club. Additionally, participation in such a club will give your teen a chance to socialize and meet new friends. Once students understand more about the mission of a service oriented club, and the side benefits of meeting new people, it could become one of the more attractive clubs in the school.

Finally, don't be afraid to mobilize other parents to make a certain club or activity the "thing to do." In other words, speak with the parents of your teen's friends behind the scenes, and together get the peer group to join a certain club together. This strategy can be a clever way to get your student, as well as the rest of their peer group, connected to the school. Remember, the important part of this isn't necessarily the club or activity your teen is involved with, but rather the simple fact that they are more involved and connected to the school. Your teen will identify with something at the school besides just going to class each day. This connection is vital to a student's overall positive high school experience.

Insider's Tip: Most fall sports and some activities (including marching band) start practices before the actual first day of school. Make sure to find out this information in the spring of your child's eighth grade year so he doesn't start behind.

"Can We Start Our Own Club?"

As a rising ninth grader, there is time to start your own club and enjoy it for several years. Most school divisions and schools have policies and regulations governing the initiation of new clubs or activities. Sometimes these clubs can be approved as "school-sponsored," or sometimes they can be approved as "Equal Access" clubs. Either way, it is a great project for your teen. This is a perfect opportunity to take on a leadership position, and, if successful, your teen will be able to enjoy the club for the next four years. Each school division has different requirements concerning the start-up of a new club or getting one approved. Sometimes the approval is left to the principal; sometimes the approval must come from the School Board. We suggest reading your school division's regulations on starting a new club and deciding if it is something your teen wants to try.

Chapter Five

Form Positive School Relationships

We must, indeed, all hang together or, most assuredly, we shall all hang separately. —Benjamin Franklin

Talk with any school "insider" and you will learn that parents who form positive school relationships with school staff enhance their teen's success at high school.

In your child's school experience, have you felt that certain students or parents get advantages? Have you felt that certain children have people looking out for them? Your feelings are probably correct. This chapter is going to give you an insider's view on how parents are able to nurture a positive relationship with the right people at the school to the benefit of their child.

Do you remember the "good old days?"

When you were a teenager, did you feel like your parents knew everything that happened to you even when they weren't present? We have heard lots of stories from parents about the "good old days" when they couldn't get away with anything because everyone knew everyone. You know how the story goes, "I couldn't act up in my hometown, because Mr. Jones would just pick up the phone and call my parents," or "When I acted up, Mr. Jones would say, 'Matthew, you better behave now because I know your brother and your parents and their cousins, and I know your pastor, too, so you better just behave so I don't have to call them.'" At least that's how the story goes. This "small town" feeling seems to be one that many people are longing for these days. In today's hectic world, school districts have a tendency to build large high schools. The personal attention seems to be gone, and the opportunity for students to get lost in the crowd has increased. But, has it really disappeared? We don't think so.

WHY ARE PERSONAL RELATIONSHIPS IMPORTANT?

When you develop relationships with the right people in your teen's high school, in a sense, you create that small town feeling where lots of folks are looking out for your teen.

As your teenager begins high school, they will long for more independence. (Remember, you did too!) There are a few key strategies for parents to use in order to survive the battle of teenage independence. (The supervision part of this battle is discussed in Chapter 6.) One of the strategies involves multiple eyes, ears, and, most importantly, establishing key adult advocates in the school for your teen. You will not be able to attend school every day with your teenager. (Of course, as principals, we tell parents that they are welcome anytime.) No matter how wonderful your child is, they act differently when they are not around you. We've seen the change in behaviors in the classroom, on the practice fields, in the hallways, at the lunch tables, at school dances, or while just hanging out with friends. Trust us; in our many years of experience in dealing with high school students, they all act differently when their parents aren't around.

Lost in the Shuffle

For years we have been telling parents of rising ninth-graders, "Don't let your child get lost in the shuffle." We felt confident with this advice until one day a parent asked a simple question, "How do I make sure that my student doesn't get 'lost in the shuffle'? What do you mean when you say that?" Our response was one that we are not proud of, "Umm, you know, don't let them get 'lost in the shuffle,' or forgotten about." Since this awkward moment, we have thought through what we mean by, "don't let your student get lost in the shuffle."

When we use that phrase, we mean that some children go

through school never making any meaningful healthy connections with the adults in high school. Research tells us that the teenagers who make at least one solid, valuable adult connection in high school are far more likely to have a positive experience in school both academically and socially. Ideally, your teen will want to make many more than just one solid relationship. For some of you, your child will make these relationships naturally. For others, you will have to take some steps to help make these relationships happen. In either case, we advocate that parents be proactive, especially in the ninth grade.

> *"No significant learning takes place without significant relationships."* —Dr. James Comer

RULES TO FORMING POSITIVE RELATIONSHIPS WITH SCHOOL STAFF

As seems to be the case with just about everything else in school, there are some not so obvious rules involved with how to form positive relationships with school staff. Here are some hints at how to ensure that you are making the best impression on those people who will have a large impact of your student's success.

The First Contact Should Be Positive

Solid relationship building, one that develops advocates not adversaries, starts on a positive level. Veteran teachers give rookie teachers this insider advice: "The best way to get parents on your side is to call all the parents of your students within the first days of school and make a positive comment about their child." The teacher should send the parent a positive message like, "Bobby is really participating well in class," or "Maria adds some very mature comments to our class discussion." Why are new teachers given this advice? Simple! All parents love to hear something positive about their teen.

Too many times the school calls only when something negative has happened. This positive phone call gives the teacher an immedi-

Heather Rosen

Students benefit greatly from forging personal relationships with faculty members. Here, a student meets with her principal to discuss school issues.

ate advocate at home. This positive contact sets the stage for cooperation so that when a teacher does have to call home about something negative, the parent is more apt to be willing to work with the teacher to solve the problem.

This same principle holds true when parents want to form positive relationships with the school staff. Teachers are human beings and, just like parents, want to hear something positive about their classes and their impact on teens. Make your first contact with a teacher positive. Send an email that says, "Hi Mr. Smith, I just wanted to drop you line to tell you how much Jimmy is enjoying your class. I appreciate your efforts. If I can be of assistance, please let me know." What you have done with this simple email is show the teacher many things: a) you and Jimmy have discussed this class at home; b) you are an involved parent and care about Jimmy's education, c) you appreciate what Mr. Smith does as a teacher, and, d) you're a supporter, not a complainer.

You have now created an advocate for your teen in that teacher's classroom. If a situation comes up where you have a concern, the teacher will be much more willing to work with you to find a positive solution. Plus, you've created a little bit of that "small town feeling" because you've made a connection with Mr. Smith. The benefits of this are immeasurable. If your teen is having any difficulty, Mr. Smith is much more likely to contact you early (knowing that you are "friendly and easy to work with") rather than letting a small problem rest, possibly to fester.

Remember, high school teachers meet anywhere from 100 to 150 students daily. They literally do not have the time to make contact with every parent every time a child may be a concern. Many times, teachers do not contact parents until the problem has gotten out of control. This fact is true whether the problem is a behavior issue or an academic one. In fact, as principals, we hear from parents all the time, "Why didn't that teacher call me earlier? If I had known, I could have done something about it!" The fact is high school teachers want to put the first responsibility for the problem on the student's shoulders in an effort to teach responsibility for one's actions. But, if you have taken the initiative to make a positive contact with the teacher, you are much more likely to be kept abreast of your student's performance in that classroom. The teacher knows you care about what happens in the classroom.

Do Not Use Email for Negative Issues

Negative issues are going to occur during the course of your teen's high school years. If you have followed the above recommendations, you have used email skillfully to nurture a positive relationship with your child's teachers. If something now comes up that is negative, you should absolutely not use email to address this issue. Many times, we have seen well-meaning parents write an email to address a negative issue that unravels all the positive feelings they have worked so hard to create. Why? People tend to write emails about potential negative issues in an emotional state. When they initially hear about a problem, instead of processing the issue, they sit down quickly at the computer and shoot off an angry email to the teacher. This form of communication should be used for positive notes or for gathering quick information. When there is a negative issue and you are thinking, "What in the world is that teacher thinking?" or "That teacher will not do that to my child," we strongly encourage you to step away from the computer and give yourself time to process how to best resolve the problem! We cannot stress this often enough.

Let's analyze why we see so many good parents, trying to do the right thing, write unpleasant, emotional emails that damage relationships at school. Email contact is still relatively new. It has been used in schools for about ten years or so depending upon where you live.

Remember back to when you were in school and you came home to your parents with a story about something negative or unfair that the teacher did? Most likely, if your parents were like ours, you probably received one of two responses. The first response might have been something like, "Well, the school makes the rules and you need to follow them. Just do what you're told," Or, if you had more responsive parents, they might have said, "I am sure that Mr. Smith has his version of what happened as well. Go talk to him tomorrow and see if you can work it out." If you really had your parents wrapped around your finger, they might sympathize with your complaint, get angry, and then plan to give the school or teacher a phone call the next day. What happened then? Everyone went to bed, slept on the issue, and calmed down. Sometimes, "sleeping on it" puts issues in their proper perspective and takes the emotional charge out of the issue.

Today, in the same scenario, a parent gets angry and instead of "sleeping on it," immediately types an email that is emotionally charged and sends it with a click of the mouse. Just like that! With email, you can't read someone's body language or tone. It is much easier to be unpleasant to someone you don't have to face. When a parent sends an email without hearing the teacher's perspective on the issue, it is very upsetting to the teacher. The teacher might not even know what incident the parents are concerned about and, responding emotionally, sends an unpleasant email right back at the parent. Before you know it, there is a ruined relationship and a negative environment for everyone.

Not only has the parent ruined the relationship with this teacher, but also it may have jeopardized the parent's reputation among several teachers. Teachers are human beings. That email might become the "talk" of the English department or the Social Studies Department. The teacher is telling other teachers, "In 25 years of teaching, I've never had a parent treat me this way!" Soon the child's other teachers hear the "legend" of the email. Then your child's teachers for the next year remember this conflict when they see your last name on their class roster. You can see the ripple effect that one mean-spirited email can have. In reality, this happens. As principals, unfortunately, we see it all the time and we spend a great deal of time trying to repair these relationships.

A former central office administrator we know advised his principals, "If you wouldn't want to read what you've said on an email on the front page of *The Washington Post,* then don't write it." His point was that when you put something in writing, such as an email, you have just created documentation. So, when you end up in the administrator's office trying to convince the principal to help you because of this unreasonable teacher, remember that the teacher has saved your emotional email and all the things you have said are documented. The teacher will use this against you to show that you are really an out-of-control parent who won't cooperate reasonably with the school.

Since the beginning of schools in America, teenagers have been "exaggerating" stories about their teachers to parents. It is a normal "right of passage." As a parent who wants to forge and keep positive relationships with school staff, make sure you take everything your high school student says with a grain of salt. Always make it a point to hear both sides of the story before reacting.

Of course, as insiders, we have seen occasions when a teacher has been unfair to a teen. The parents who gather all the facts and deal with the issues on the phone or, better yet, at a face-to-face conference, are the ones who resolve the concern correctly. These parents get the results they want without ruining the positive relationship with the school.

> *Insider's Tip: Savvy parents skillfully take steps to create their own "small town feeling" for their child. These parents foster the positive relationships at the school that help their teen be successful.*

Do Not Go Overboard or Smother

Once you have established a positive relationship with the school staff, don't go overboard. As stated before, teachers and other school personnel deal with many students every day. You have already made a savvy move by making sure your student is receiving positive attention. Overdoing it could have a negative effect. You may transition from being a helpful, caring, involved parent to an overbearing, pain-in-the-neck parent. Do not expect to have daily or even weekly contact with school personnel. The amount of contact will depend upon how your teen is doing. If your teen is struggling academically or behaviorally, then we encourage more regular contacts.

Short Follow-up Notes Are Very Effective
(Especially to Say, "Thank You.")

When you are working with a school staff member, make sure you always send a quick follow-up note to bring the matter to a satisfactory conclusion. These shouldn't be long communications, but they are necessary. Whatever the issue might be, taking two minutes to write a "thank you" note or email to the teacher, administrator, secretary, coach, school nurse, or guidance counselor can go miles toward getting future help. These folks are going to remember you as a grateful, positively involved parent. Therefore, when your teen might need assistance again, they will go out of their way to help. Again, you have taken another step in creating your own "small town feeling" for your child.

Follow-up notes (especially those of thanks) should be genuine. Wait for a legitimate event to happen that allows you to send a follow-up note. Don't force the issue. Otherwise, school staff will recognize it as forced, and it won't have the same impact.

Treat School Staff as Partners

A key ingredient in forming positive school relationships with school staff is treating every person with the dignity he or she deserves. Every member of the school's staff must be treated as an equal and valuable partner in getting your teen through high school successfully.

When issues do arise, you do not help solve the problem by blaming school staff. If you have a teacher conference and approach the teacher with the attitude that the teacher must be doing something wrong or is unreasonably demanding because your teen is struggling, you will put the school staff on the defensive. They will then spend the entire meeting trying to salvage their reputation rather than looking for solutions to help your child. Conversely, if you approach the conference with the attitude that we all (parent, teacher, and student) must work together for the success of your teen, that is exactly what will happen.

Working together with school staff as partners will positively impact every aspect of your teen's high school experience. Quite honestly, many people must work together to help your child; this partnership is truly important. Your handling of these relationships is paramount to your teen's success.

As we have stated many times in this book, school staff are human beings. Human beings want to help people when they are treated well, thanked, and made to feel they are making a positive difference in someone's life. On the other hand, human beings don't want to help someone if they are blamed, told how to do their job, treated in a condescending manner, or just plain made to feel unappreciated.

Be Careful in the Neighborhood

One pitfall for many well-meaning parents is the neighborhood gossip mill. If you want to develop and maintain positive relationships with school staff, you must stay clear of the "mother's mafia." Trust us, these folks' reputations precede them, and school staff is well aware of the things that are being said in the neighborhood.

Let us give you an example. You're at a social gathering in your neighborhood on a Saturday night. You are with a group of parents, one of whom thinks he is the resident "school expert" in the neighborhood because he volunteers at the school. Several of the parents begin bad-mouthing a particular teacher. The conversation turns to you because everyone knows your fourteen-year-old just started at the high school. To avoid an awkward moment, you innocently say, "High school is definitely different from middle school; the teachers don't seem as friendly, and I don't know the principal yet."

Someone might misconstrue what you have just said as negative, and it will get back to school staff. The volunteer might tell someone at the school, "Mrs. Jones really doesn't like any of her child's teachers, and she thinks the principal is aloof and isolated." Well, you know what happens. That someone will tell someone, who will tell someone else, and eventually, it will get back to your child's teachers.

Negative, unhappy people want others to be negative and unhappy. Stay positive about your teen's school and confident in your child's teachers. As a savvy parent, who wants to do the best for your teen, you want to be known as a supportive parent. Don't do damage to the relationships you have built at the school because of a slip of the tongue in the neighborhood. Remember, even your best friend can inadvertently contribute to rumors. The only person completely looking out for your teen is you.

FIVE IMPORTANT PEOPLE WITH WHOM TO FORM A POSITIVE RELATIONSHIP OTHER THAN THE TEACHERS

By far, teachers are the most important group with whom to form positive relationships. Day in and day out, teachers will have the greatest impact on your teen. The following people, however, can also help your teen's successful transition to high school. Positive relationships with these folks will pay great dividends in helping your teen and will provide support to you as a parent.

- **Guidance counselor.** Your teen's guidance counselor will directly impact your child in many ways. The guidance counselor is likely to play many roles in your teen's high school career. For example, some roles include scheduling the right classes for your child, helping resolve teacher conflicts, and assisting with social problems. Maybe most importantly, the guidance counselor will be the chief guide in helping your teen apply to colleges and/or preparing for life after high school. A sad secret in U.S. high schools is that most guidance departments are understaffed; thus, counselors serve too many students to properly help each child. The savviest parents form a relationship with the guidance counselor to make sure their teen receives the individual attention deserved.
- **Your teen's coach/club sponsor.** Graduating seniors will often recognize a coach, club sponsor, or activity sponsor as the most influential adult in their school lives over the past four years. This person can be a tremendous advocate for your teen in times of trouble and can be an extra set of eyes and ears to look after your child. The coach/sponsor will most likely see your teen outside of the classroom setting; thus, he or she will have a different perspective on your child's development.
- **School secretaries.** School insiders will tell you that often it appears as if the secretaries are the ones really running the school. While we know this isn't true as far as what's happening in the classroom, we can tell you, as principals, we rely heavily on this skilled group of professionals to make our schools run efficiently. Having a positive relationship with the secretarial group will make your and your teen's school life so much better. Make sure you and your teen are always respectful in your interactions with this group. Say "thank you" and be appreciative of any help they provide. Send them a small gift or nice note on Administrative Professional's Day. Forming a positive relationship with these folks can be extremely beneficial.
- **Athletic director/activities director (AD).** If your teen is involved in any sport or club, the AD plays a major role in these

activities. Behind the scenes, this person is responsible for making sure that the extra-curricular life of the school runs smoothly. The AD is likely to have an important, but often unrecognized, impact on your teen. ADs work with coaches, set tryout procedures, and make sure students are treated fairly when participating in extra-curricular activities at your school. If you have a problem with a coach or another related issue, the AD is a great person to have in your corner.

- **Your child's administrator and/or principal.** Depending on the size of your school, your teen will either know the principal well or, in a large school, will be assigned an assistant principal by alphabet or grade level. Most parents prefer that the administrator not know their teen because they view this as a negative. Honestly, we disagree. We have formed numerous positive relationships with parents and students. Administrators, like guidance counselors, deal with many students daily. Anything you can do as a parent to help your teen get recognized (in a positive way) will pay off in the future.

  Although it is unusual, we have had savvy parents meet with us over the summer preceding their child's ninth grade year to introduce us to their teen. July and early August are good times for this introduction, as the principal's schedule tends to be much less hectic. Simply call the principal's administrative assistant to set up a brief ten– to fifteen-minute meeting. This meeting is likely to pay dividends some time down the road.

- **Bonus person: school nurse (if your child has medical issues/severe allergies).** Many high schools have a school nurse assigned to them. If your child has severe allergies or medical issues, make a plan to form a positive relationship with the school nurse. School divisions have rules about students bringing medicine to school (even over-the-counter medicine or prescription medicine). Meet the school nurse and make sure you and your teen are complying with all the proper procedures with regard to these issues. The school nurse should be made aware of your child's specific medical issues and, together, you need to develop an emergency medical treatment plan. By developing a positive relationship with the school nurse, you have one more person to keep an eye on your teen in the "small town" you have masterfully developed to promote your child's success.

Chapter Six

All Teenagers Need Supervision

Nothing good happens after midnight.   —Edward J. Healey, Sr.

When we discuss ninth grade transitions with educators, one of the first things they say is "Make sure to tell parents that they have to supervise their child." When we discuss proper supervision with parents, we hear, "My kid's a good kid; he'll be okay," or "My child won't listen to me; I can't control who she is with and what she is doing." These types of discussions often lead us to recount a story we heard previously from one of our recent high school graduates.

> *When I finally turned eighteen-years-old in the spring of my senior year of high school, I was so excited. I had been waiting for years to be able to say I was an adult. Finally, I knew that I was in charge of my life and could make decisions that for years my parents made for me.*
>
> *My parents were really pretty excited too. They talked about me "paying my own bills," and "moving out and getting my own job." I could tell though that deep down, my parents didn't want me to go anywhere. They knew I would be going to college in a few months and I think they were anxious about me leaving.*
>
> *I thought I had it made. I was eighteen, and an adult! My parents were overall pretty flexible. I mean, here I was, eating their food, my mom was doing my laundry, and I was coming and going quite often with my job, my friends, and my activities. So finally, I was an adult, getting ready to graduate high school, I had already been accepted into a top university, and in*

general, life was good.

Then I did it. The first Saturday night after my eighteenth birthday arrived, and I went out with my friends. Now that I was eighteen, I assumed I was in charge of my life, and didn't have to worry about any previous curfew established by my parents. In my mind, things were different now. I was an adult. I had worked hard to be successful. My parents were proud of me. I deserved to be given some freedom.

To my surprise, when I arrived home well after the midnight curfew my parents established for me at the beginning of my senior year, my parents were sitting at the kitchen table waiting for me! My mom was crying; my dad was yelling. It was clear by the end of our discussion that if I expected to live in their house, I had to play by their rules no matter what age. The next day, after the battle, when everyone had a chance to sleep and calm down, my dad explained it to me in simple terms. "Nothing good happens after midnight. After midnight is when good people make bad decisions."

As we reflect on this story now, we realize that this eighteen-year-old, even as an adult, got a strong dose of reality. His parents were still in control, still had certain expectations, and still knew bad things could happen if you put a good person in the wrong place at the wrong time. Teenagers don't believe this; they believe that they are in control of every situation they are in and should be in charge of their own life. In reality, they are still learning how to become adults and need guidelines, boundaries, and supervision. It is a parent's job to set these boundaries. The culture set in this young man's house had been made clear since childhood. The parents were in charge and all throughout high school nothing changed, even after his eighteenth birthday.

Insider's Tip: The bad news is . . . Your job is never done.
The good news is . . . Your job is never done.

Virginia Hamrick

Establishing clear rules at the beginning of the year with your teen sets clear expectations for behavior as he or she enters the ninth grade year.

OKAY, HERE'S THE BAD NEWS

Often, we have encountered parents who believe they have reached the finish line when their child has finished middle school. Admittedly, middle school can be filled with exasperating times for parents. You have had to accept that your teen doesn't want you around all the time. Your kid's friends seem to be more important to your child than you are. The good news is that by the end of high school, your teen will mature and make you feel proud, provided you gave proper supervision at the beginning, at the middle, and the end of high school. As high school insiders, we have seen skillful parents develop strategies to help shepherd their student through their high school years. Based on our experiences, here are our suggestions for your consideration as you begin this journey.

Suggestions on How to Continue Your Job as a Parent

Have Clear Rules for School Nights and Weekends. Know Where Your Child Is After School

As a new high school student, your fourteen-year-old is afforded all sorts of new freedoms. However, all ninth grade students need to have clear boundaries set with regard to certain social freedoms. Some clear rules follow:

- You should establish a curfew for your ninth grade student on the weekends and school nights.
- Under most circumstances, do not allow your ninth grader to go to any weekend "get-togethers" with eleventh and twelfth-graders. These "get-togethers" are most likely parties. If your teen tells you the parents of the host student will be home during this "get-together," you should absolutely call that parent beforehand to find out more about the event. Your child might be embarrassed, but the parents will completely understand and appreciate your call.
- Be wary of "sleepovers" in high school. These events often deteriorate late at night after well-meaning parents have gone to bed. Verify with the parents of the house that there will be supervision.
- After school dismissal, you need to know exactly where your student is, whom they are with, and what they are doing. The time between school dismissal and when parents arrive home from work is the most unsupervised time in the country.

Have Routine Talks With Your Child About Your Expectations

Research says that during the teenage years, a teen's friends and parents have the greatest influence over decisions they make. The problem is that your teen is going to pretend to disagrees with you or will act like they are not listening to you most of the time. Trust the research and us; they are listening to everything you say. Make sure your routine talks include your expectations and consequences if your teen does not meet your expectations.

> *Insider's Tip: Research clearly says that one way to lower the risk of your teen's chance of alcohol abuse, drug abuse, and other dangerous behaviors is to eat dinner together routinely as a family.*

Be Your Child's Parent, Not Friend

High school students have many friends in their lives. As much as we all want to "relate" to kids and be the "cool" mom or dad, what kids really want and need are parents who set boundaries, have high expectations, and have unconditional love for their child whether they are popular or have a bad day. The following example is based on a real conference we had with a student and his parents.

> *Andrew turned fifteen years old during January of his freshman year. He had been a pretty good student during his middle school years, but now he was sitting with his parents and the principal in a meeting discussing his lack of academic success.*
>
> *"Mr. and Mrs. Ross; are you aware that Andrew is late for his first period class, a class he is failing, just about every day?"*
>
> *Andrew's dad responded, "Well he gets a ride with the son of our next door neighbor. He's a senior, and he's always running late."*
>
> *"So, why don't you have him ride the bus? He'll be on time everyday."*
>
> *Andrew's mom said, "Well, he really doesn't want to ride the bus, and we can't get him up that early."*
>
> *"Why not?"*
>
> *"Well, he stays up late at night texting his friends, playing video games, or watching TV. When his alarm goes off, he just won't get out of bed."*

Gregory Johnston

Even though it may seem at times that your teen isn't listening to you, it is important that you remember that your influence is the most important factor in the decisions your teen makes.

Getting teenagers to go to bed and get up early for school is not a new problem. Making excuses for them and, as parents, sending signals that this behavior is acceptable is new. This story is a clear example of parents who are afraid or unwilling to take a stand over a simple problem and the solution. The problem, being late for school, if not corrected during the freshman year, will only get worse as the student gets older. Students realize when parents do not have control over their behavior. What is worse, in this specific case, is that Andrew witnessed his parents making excuses for him to the school principal. The result was that the school's ability to help these parents take a strong position in their efforts to manage their student's behavior was greatly diminished.

Let's see how this might have gone better. Instead of making a weak excuse for their teen's bad decisions, what if the parents had immediately agreed with the principal that it made perfect sense for their teen to ride the bus each day. What the student will have witnessed in this case was that the school and his parents were aligned as a team to develop solutions to his behavioral problems. This strategy will not only help to solve the immediate problem, but also will encourage both the school and the parents to seek each other out in dealing with any future issues.

Know Your Child's Friends

High school usually brings a whole new set of people to whom your teen has not been exposed. Not all of these people are going to have the same goals and aspirations that you have for your child. Not all of these kids will have parents that are as concerned and involved as you are. We cannot emphasize enough how important it is to know who your teen is with and where your child is at all times.

One family we work with sets very clear boundaries for their daughter and her older boyfriend. The parents have tried on multiple occasions to contact the boyfriend's parents to get to know them. The parents want to be sure that the expectations and rules for their daughter are shared by her boyfriend's parents. To their frustration, the boyfriend's parents have not called them back. These parents have handled it beautifully. They know that, if they forbid their daughter from seeing the boy, she will rebel and try to sneak out to see him. Instead these parents let their daughter see the boy, but she is not allowed to go to his house until they speak with his parents. The boyfriend is welcome at their house and for approved outings with strict curfews, but their daughter knows she is not allowed at his house. They have clearly explained to her the consequences if she violates their wishes.

We cannot emphasize how important it is to be familiar with your teen's friends. Face-to-face meetings with your child's new high school friends can tell you much about their character. Are they respectful of adults? Your house? Do they make eye contact with you? Be extremely concerned if your teen becomes friends with older students. Ninth- graders really have little business socializing with juniors or seniors in high school. These types of relationships can open up dangerous avenues for your teen, including: 1) the dangers associated with being in a car with a teenage driver; 2) exposure to high school parties (including the drugs and alcohol associated with these parties); 3) early pressure to engage in sexual activity; and, 4) in some cases, a negative attitude toward school.

> *Insider's Tip: If your ninth grade student begins to socialize outside of the school setting with eleventh and twelfth grade students, you should be very concerned.*

Don't Let Your Children Compare You to Other Parents

Inevitably, there will be parents of one of your child's friends who let their teen stay out to all hours, or let their teen go to "parties" with seniors. If your teen tries to compare you to these parents, the purpose is to use peer pressure to make you be irresponsible. You have to make the best decision for your child. Period. Do not worry what other parents think. Do not worry when your teen says, "My life will be ruined!" because you don't think "hanging out" at the mall is a good idea. The following is a true story from a suburban middle class neighborhood. It is a story about two kids who convinced their parents that everyone lets their ninth grader "hang out" at the mall and go to the movies unsupervised.

> *Shane and Bobby were two fourteen-year-old ninth grade students. One Saturday, they told their parents they were going to "hang out" at the mall and see a movie. Shane's dad dropped them off and told them that he would be back in three hours to pick them up. Of course, Shane and Bobby never had plans to see any movie. They had heard that the mall is where you could buy marijuana and, in fact, knew two seniors from their school who dealt marijuana at the mall. After 30 minutes of walking around and doing nothing, Shane and Bobby finally found the two seniors. The seniors told them the stuff was in their car in the parking lot, and all four boys went to the car. Shane and Bobby got in the back seat as the two older boys got in the front*

> *seat. Shane asked, "How much?"*
> *One of the older boys said, "Everything you got."*
> *Shane replied, "What? What do you mean, 'everything we've got'?"*
> *The older boy said, "I mean everything you got."*
> *With this statement the older boy pulled out a gun and pointed it at the two younger boys. The older boys punched the younger boys several times, and Shane and Bobby handed over their wallets. The older boys threw the two ninth-graders out of the car and drove off.*

Don't go against your instincts because your teen pressures you by saying that other parents are letting their kids do things. Remember that ninth-grade students are fourteen- and fifteen-year-old children who should not be "hanging out" unsupervised by adults. They need to have a curfew; you need to know where they are, with whom they are spending time, and what they are doing. Trust us, many other parents feel the same way you do, but they give in to the peer pressure.

Give Fair, Consistent, and Reasonable Consequences for Violations

Good teens (even the "straight A" students) need supervision and must face consequences when warranted. Your teen may do many things right, but if your expectations haven't be met, there must be accountability. If you make threats of punishment and then do not follow through, a teenager will quickly realize that you are not committed to enforcing the rules. Soon, the small violations may turn into big ones, and then bigger ones, and eventually, maybe, life-changing problems.

On the other hand, keep your teen's violations in perspective. If you overreact to small infractions, then if they do something really big, you'll have nothing left. For example, let's say you allow your teen to attend a high school dance. You tell your child that you will be outside the school at 10:30 pm to provide a ride home. You arrive at 10:25 pm and end up waiting 20 minutes. This situation means that consequences are in order, but there is no need to ban your teen from attending any more school dances during the next four years of high school. Rather, a more appropriate punishment is for you to inform your teen that the next time they want to stay at a school function they will be required to leave the function 20 minutes early. Then, remember to enforce this consequence!

Here is one quick side note about the dancing at high school dances. Recently, the style of dancing has become a whole new concern. Schools handle the dancing of students in different ways, but left unchecked, the dancing can be extremely inappropriate. It might be a good idea to discuss with your teen what kind of dancing is appropriate at these functions.

> *Insider's Tip: Volunteer to chaperone the first dance of your child's ninth grade year. A school that attempts to monitor student dancing will welcome you, and you will get a firsthand look at what students are doing at school dances. If your school resists your efforts to volunteer, that should be a red flag warning you about school dance behavior.*

When giving your ninth-grader consequences for behavior, keep it all in perspective. Try not to give consequences when you are angry and emotional. Don't feel pressured to dole out immediate consequences after your teen violates a rule. Tell your child clearly that the rules have been violated, that you still love them, but you are disappointed. Tell your child that you will discuss the consequences in the morning when everyone has had a chance to sleep on it.

Most likely a good night's sleep will put things in perspective for you. If you wake up still angry with your teen, then it may be a serious issue. If you wake up realizing the violation was not that big a deal, you still need to give a consequence, but one that fits the degree of the violation. When your teen violates your trust, it is a big deal, but how you handle it now could have long-lasting effects (positive and negative).

Be Careful With Your Child's Use of Technology

A teen having unsupervised access to the internet can create a huge problem. It is not only a concern because of the abundance of pornography and the number of child predators in the online world, but also, a huge problem because of the damage kids do to each other on social websites such as Facebook™ or MySpace™. We strongly encourage you to insist that your teen accept you as a "friend" on his or her Facebook™ or MySpace™ page. This should not be optional. If your teen tells you that they do not have such a social networking page, go online and search for yourself. It is pretty easy to use, and it is foolish not to check up on your child's online world.

We, as school officials, use those pages to better understand potential problems in school. Many students have inappropriate pictures or descriptions of themselves on their online profiles. Students will say nasty, threatening words to one another if they are angry. Child predators search these pages looking for vulnerable targets.

There are many amazing uses for the internet and certainly information is at this generation's fingertips like never before. We recognize some of what teenagers do on Facebook™ and MySpace™ is harmless; and that many will benefit from online socialization and community building. The important lesson here is that you as parents must supervise the online world just as you do the real world. It can be just as dangerous. Your teen may not understand that the precautions you take are to ensure everyone's safety. Your teen may say it is an invasion of privacy. Rationally explain to your child why you are concerned, but be vigilant.

Certainly, another prevalent technology is mobile phones. As school administrators, it seems that every single teenager uses mobile technology. Here are a few things to consider regarding your teen's cell phone use. Virtually every cell phone comes with a camera. We highly recommend that you look at your child's photographs on the camera periodically without giving them warning. In our experience, students who are involved in illegal or inappropriate activities, often take pictures of it. We're not sure why they do this, but they do. We've seen drug and alcohol use, crimes committed, violence, nudity, and sexual content on the cell phones of high school students. In fact, we have even had cases where students took pictures of other students, without their knowledge, in locker rooms and bathrooms! Parents should also be aware that cell phones, IPOD's, etc., have become targets for thieves in schools.

The new trend with camera phones is to take pictures of tests and assignments for the purposes of cheating. As you can imagine, this practice is extremely troubling to teachers and administrators. In fact, this concern is becoming a nationwide issue at high schools and colleges. It is important for students and parents to know that many college applications specifically ask if a student has been caught cheating, or disciplined for academic violations or dishonesty. The consequences of these actions almost always negatively impact the student's high school grades at the time of the offense, then come back to bite them again when the students is ready to begin applying to colleges. Many freshmen don't understand the lasting impact of the impulse decision to use their phones in this manner. Having a quick conversation with your freshman about this issue may save great embarrassment and trouble down the road.

Make it clear to your child that cell phones should not be used during school hours. This restriction includes text messaging and calls from friends. As the parent, do not call or text message your child on their cell phone during the school day. Doing so sends a mixed-message to your teen regarding the importance of following school rules. If there is an emergency, or you need to get a message to your child, there is always someone at school in who will deliver a message from a parent or guardian.

OKAY, HERE'S THE GOOD NEWS . . .

Deep down, really deep down, you don't want your job as a parent to be completed when your teen enters high school. High school can be a rewarding, challenging, and fun time of life. Parents can be a major part of this time. Just as we've learned from our savvy parents on how

Friday night football games are great chances to experience the high school culture along with your teen. These are often fun community events.

to manage their children's behavior and set boundaries, we see how these same parents capitalize on the rewards, challenges, and important moments in their teen's high school life. These parents are truly a part of their children's high school experience. The following five suggestions will make "supervision" a positive experience for you and your child.

Attend Many "Big Events" Along With Your Child

Say your daughter wants to go to the first football game of the year. The first football game of the year for a ninth-grader is usually an important social event. She may pretend to want to see the game, but in reality she wants to talk with her friends, see who is there and be seen by others, and, in general, be a kid. This activity is healthy and worthy, and you should encourage your teen to attend. However, this encouragement does not mean that dropping her off at the school and picking her up four hours later is the right thing to do. We suggest instead that you consider attending the game along with your daughter. This decision will help you get a feel for the atmosphere at the school's extracurricular activities, watch what other kids do, and let you see how the school administration provides a safe, secure environment. This suggestion does not mean you need to be at your daughter's side the entire night. Arrive with her, tell her where you will be seated, and tell her where to meet you at the end of the game. Honestly, your daughter may not even look at you or speak to you once during the game, but she'll know you are there.

One hint with this endeavor: Don't give your daughter any money. She'll have to find you if she gets thirsty or hungry and it can be a natural, unplanned mid-point check-in time. Once you experience the initial game or event, get together with her friends' parents. Each of you can then take turns bringing the kids to events so you don't have to go every single time. We believe the excitement associated with high school sports is unparalleled, and that you will have a great time while supporting the school and being a savvy parent. We understand, however, that you cannot attend every event.

Always (If Possible) Attend Events in Which Your Child Participates

If your teen is participating in a certain activity or sport, do *not* miss these events. Even if your child acts like these events are not important for you to attend or tells you that it doesn't matter if you attend, your involvement is important and does matter. Here's a story from one student whom we know well.

When I played baseball (or other various sports) growing up, my parents never missed a game. Never. As I became a teenager, however, instead of my dad's coaching and my mom's hugging during games when I was upset, I distanced myself from them. My parents wanted to take pictures of me in the dugout. My mom wanted to give me a kiss for good luck before the games. My dad wanted to call me over for strategic suggestions. With each passing year, I became more and more resistant. In fact, sometimes I was downright rude to them. I ignored them. I rolled my eyes. I would say, "Leave me alone!" After games, I would tell my parents not to embarrass me in front of my friends. My mom would feel pretty awful, and sometimes I made her cry.

When I was sixteen, I was playing baseball on the JV squad for my high school. It was the last game of a long season. In this particular game, I was playing second base. It was a tie game; the other team had a runner on third base with one out. The batter hit a sky-high fly ball about 20 to 25 feet behind second base. I went back behind second base and made a diving catch falling to the ground. The runner on third based tagged up and ran for home. I jumped to my feet and fired a perfect throw to the catcher at home. The catcher tagged the runner out, and we made it out of a tight inning. It may have been one of the best defensive plays I had ever made in baseball. When I ran to the dugout, I looked to the stands. My parents weren't there. For the first time in my sporting career, they did not come to my game. I was devastated.

When I got home, I yelled at my mom and dad, "Where were you?"

"We didn't think you wanted us there." That was the last organized baseball game I played.

As a parent of a high school student, your need to accept that your teen is going to tell you all sorts of things they don't mean. Trust us, teenage students want their parents to witness and share in their performances every bit as much as their younger counterparts. They want to know that you love them whether they drop the ball or hit a homerun. Go to every event you can, but don't take it personally if your existence goes unacknowledged. Be aware of what your teen does at these events without smothering him or her. Don't be loud or obnoxious. Don't argue with referees or yell at the coach. Be there to support your child and the team.

At high school graduations, we have heard hundreds of high

school seniors recount the incredible impact their parents had on their development. Much of the teens' evidence of support was simply the fact that their parents always attended their children's sports, concerts, or club events. This involvement was usually passive. The parents were simply there to watch and support their child. We can tell you that teens notice and appreciate this support. Believe it or not, one day your child may even thank you for always being there!

Talk About School with Your Child

As simple as this suggestion sounds, it is amazing how many parents don't engage in this important conversation with their children. Kids today are learning some highly sophisticated and interesting topics in school, and they might even be studying some of the same material you did when you were in high school.

Remember when your five-year-old went off to kindergarten? When your child came home, you wanted to hear about every second of the day. Nothing should be different now. Despite their telling you they didn't learn anything that day, we can tell you their day is interesting, fun, and full of great learning opportunities.

> *Insider's Tip: If you are having trouble discussing what your teen is doing in classes, feel free to email the teacher. Effective teachers should be happy to provide you with some "inside information" that can help you get the conversation started at home.*

Be Interested in Your Child's Discussions About Other Kids

After working with teenagers for many years, we have found that one of the constants is that they love to socialize. They all experience high school "drama" of some sort. Encourage these discussions by first asking about other students whom you have known previously, "How's Brandy enjoying high school?" or "Do you ever see Luke at school?" Little prompts such as these can stimulate your teen into a whole discussion about interesting information you want to know.

> *Insider's Tip: Savvy parents don't force these types of conversations with their teenager, but rather create an environment at home where the teen feels comfortable talking about their friends. Sometimes teenagers don't feel like talking. It will only make things worse by "making" them talk. Savvy parents manufacture opportunities (dinner, car rides, etc.), that provide a venue for these types of discussions. When your teenager wants to talk, you must focus your attention on him and stop the other things you are doing.*

At times, adults dismiss this information. On the other hand, you should be careful not to overreact every time your teen tells you someone "said something about someone." Rather, this is a critical time to just listen to your child. If you muddle through all the silliness about kids liking each other or looking mean at someone, you will be able to pick up some subtle yet important information about your teen's transition to high school.

If your teen brings up names you have never heard, make sure to ask more questions. Try to ask these probing questions in a gentle, non-threatening manner. In other words, ask the questions out of curiosity rather than in an accusatory nature. In reality, you're gathering information, but your child needs to know your actively listening because you care. Inside you may be thinking, "Oh my goodness, I'm never letting my teen go over to that kid's house." To your child it is better if you say, "Really, he used those bad words when speaking to his parents. Wow." You might also follow up with something like, "What do you think about the way he spoke to his parents?"

Remember, the key to these discussions is not to get mad at your teen because of something another child did. If you start to make these judgments, your teen will learn quickly not to discuss these things with you anymore.

IN SUMMARY

Whether or not you subscribe to some of the specific suggestions we have provided in this chapter, the most important thing you should realize is that every teenager wants and needs behavior boundaries. As career educators who have worked exclusively with high-school-age students, it has become clear (sometimes painfully so) that every child needs this guidance. The worst thing you can do as a parent with a ninth grade student is to bury your head in the sand when problems arise (no matter how minor) and not address them in some way. Too many times we have seen parents dismiss problems by saying, "My kid will grow up and mature." This response does happen in some cases, but many times, the problems get much worse and have life-altering consequences.

Chapter Seven

Progress Monitoring: Keeping an Eye on Your Student's Progress to Avoid "Big Issues"

We hear the following story from parents all too often:

> *We thought everything was going great! Every day when Kyle came home from school, we would ask him, "How did everything go" and he'd say, "It was okay." He would go to his room and disappear for several hours, later saying that he was doing his homework. We didn't hear anything from school, so we figured, "No news is good news." When we received his report card our jaws dropped—three Cs and two D+s! Kyle had always been an A or B student! How did we get into this mess without knowing anything was wrong? Why hadn't we heard from school?*

You might be thinking, "This happens often?!?" In fact, it does. A high school student can earn all Cs and Ds on a report card and stay completely "off the radar". You have to remember that a typical high school teacher could have nearly 150 students; 20 of those may be failing! Teachers often spend the majority of their time addressing the issues of failing students. C and D students are at least passing! The teacher may very well assume that C and D grades are the norm for this student, especially since the parent has never made contact. It may surprise and disappoint you, but it is a very realistic and common situation. Don't let it happen to you. You can avoid this situation by monitoring the progress of your freshman right from the start.

If you have ever spent time on the water with veteran mariners, you may have heard them say that no matter how calm the water is and no matter how much fun everyone is having, the captain must always "keep a weather eye open." What they mean is that, if you are vigilant and observant, you will be able to see problems coming well before they become serious and unmanageable. At sea, being surprised by bad weather is the last thing you want to have happen.

As the "captain" of your freshman through the ninth grade year, you must also "keep a weather eye open." Many of the issues that give freshmen parents concerns start off as small and manageable problems that can be quickly and easily solved or avoided if recognized and dealt with promptly. Savvy parents carefully monitor the progress of their teen and are able to recognize potential problems and avoid them before they get too serious.

> *Insider's Tip: Your freshman will sometimes resent your progress monitoring. They will perceive it as mistrust or "babying." Don't worry about it. They need you to keep watch over their social, emotional, and academic lives more than ever. An ounce of prevention is worth a pound of cure.*

Parents often think, "Our kid is in high school now. Shouldn't we be backing off and letting him do this on his own?" Our answer is an emphatic, "No!" The fourteen- and fifteen-year-olds coming into their ninth grade year need layers of support and guidance from their parents and families. They may say, "Mom, don't worry about it. I can handle it." But the truth is that they often don't know where to start to begin to address their problems. At this stage is where you come in.

There will be any number of ways to keep track of your student. It is important that you let your freshman know, right from the start, that you will remain a part of school life just as you were in middle school. Some parents monitor their student's progress in secret, and when they finally step in to help their student manage an issue, it appears to their teen that they have been "spying" on them. Don't let this happen. You are in charge! Let your child know what information you will be seeking and how you will be finding it. Let them know that you'll be watching and will be involved. This alone may save you from some problems down the road as your teen will be less likely to let things slide. They will know that you'll be watching.

Here are some ways to "keep your weather eye open" for your student:

- **Register for your school's online parent information system.** Many schools have an online student management system that allows parents to see everything that is recorded electronically for their student. From each teacher's gradebook to daily attendance, you will find that this is the most powerful and effective way to keep track of your student's school performance. We cannot stress this approach enough. Savvy parents use this system more than their student would ever expect. It is a valuable resource for monitoring the progress of your student.

    We have one additional note about this method. If your school uses a system such as the one described above, find out from the teacher how often it is updated. In many cases the attendance data are "real time" while the grades may get updated once a week. It's best you find out this information ahead of time because your student will use excuses like, "It's not updated yet," or "The teacher accidentally marked me tardy, I wasn't really tardy." Remember the old adage, "Trust, but verify."

- **Make sure you are on your school's email distribution list.** Most schools now send communications electronically. These updates/newsletters are written to inform the community of upcoming events, issues, news, and concerns as they arise.

- **Have daily conversations about what is going on at school over dinner.** Don't let your student reply, "Nothing." when you ask, "What happened at school today?" Dig deeper and find out what they are studying in classes and ask how the teacher is going to assess this knowledge. Through this practice you will find out about big projects, essays, and upcoming tests. You should be seeing your teen working on these projects and studying for these tests. The research on having dinner as a family is startling. Without a doubt this is a practice you should make part of your family routine.

- **Check your student's daily planner every day.** (See Chapter 3.) This check is the easiest way to keep track of upcoming assignments and enables you to monitor your student's organizational skills. Use the planner as a springboard to help your student develop timelines and schedules for work completion.

- **Consider asking for progress report each week.** Many schools have a "Weekly Progress Report" form for students who are struggling so that students and parents can get frequent feedback about how the student has done in class that week. If you suspect that your teen is struggling in a class, you may want to use this resource. Students generally ask each teacher to assess their performance and behavior, and to note any concerns (missing assignments, low test or quiz grades, etc.).

- **Contact teachers directly by email.** If you want the fastest response, send your child's teacher an email. The best approach is to ask specific questions and let the teacher know that he or she can send you very simple and brief answer. If you want more specifics or information, ask for them in a follow-up email, but be careful not to start an "email war" with your teen's teacher. For best results, set up a face-to-face meeting with the teacher. (See "Chapter 9 for advice on how to meet with teachers.)

- **Beware the zero.** The absolutely number one reason many freshmen and their parents have "report card sticker shock" is the damage caused by a missing assignment, project, or test, which can affect the overall grade average in a class. High school teachers believe that it is the student's responsibility to contact the teacher about work missed when they have been absent from class. As a parent, we highly suggest you limit your stu-

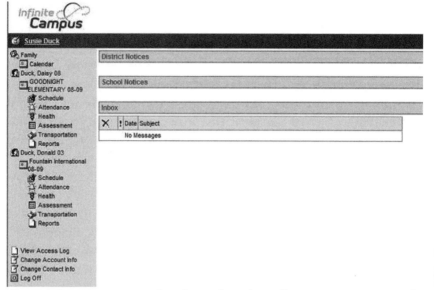

Infinite Campus

Parent information systems, such as the one shown here, allow parents to access up-to-date information about their teen's grades, attendance, assignments, and other pieces of excellent data for progress monitoring.

dent's absences from class (especially in core subjects). When your teen must be absent from class, we recommend contacting the teacher to get make up or missed work be a top priority.

Insider's Tip: Don't start "email wars" with teachers. Not only will you lose (even if you win in the short term, your child will lose in the long term), but also you may become the "topic of the day" in the teacher's lounge. Ideally, set up a face-to-face conference with the teacher and approach the issue in a positive manner.

These are all great ways for you to monitor the progress of your ninth grader. All of them can be very useful in gathering the information you need to help guide and shepherd your teen through what can be a difficult and challenging year. We encourage you to use all of these methods, plus any more you develop, or ones that your individual school makes available to you to keep track of how your student is transitioning to high school.

It is important to give a word of advice and warning: There is a fine line between appropriate progress monitoring for your student and becoming what educators now call "helicopter parents". The former are viewed by your student's teachers and administrators as concerned and aware parents who are supporting both the student and the school by ensuring that their teen is staying on track for success as a freshman. The latter are seen as smothering, overbearing nuisances who hover over their child to the detriment of their development.

Here are some ideas on how to be a supportive parent, monitoring the progress of your teen without becoming overbearing:

- **Don't overwhelm your student's teachers with requests for updates.** Between the teacher's syllabus, the online parent information system, and your student's feedback, you should be able to gather most of the information you need to stay on top of your student's progress. Only contact the teacher when you are really worried or confused about your teen's success in class.
- **Don't be a fixer.** Your job as the parent of a freshman is not to make your student's problems go away. Your job is to help your teen recognize problems as they arise and assist in developing solutions. Allow your student to deal with teachers directly without you as the intermediary. You should get directly involved only after all other methods have been exhausted.
- **Don't "jump on" every issue that arises.** Your teen doesn't need you to harp on every missed assignment, every low grade, or every class tardy that is received. Be judicious in your constructive criticism. Let your child have some breathing room to find his or her own way in school. But stay aware. You need to step in when the issues develop into problems that need your direct attention.

The bottom line is that the ninth-grade year is too important to your teen's future to be left up to chance. Your fourteen- or fifteen-year-old child will continue to need your loving guidance and support to stay on track and make the progress necessary to reach those goals. Keeping watch over the progresses your student is making through the daily and weekly grind as a high school student will be trying, but helping your students avoid finding themselves in a serious academic hole is the reward for the diligent and vigilant parent.

Chapter Eight

My Kid's Grades Stink!
What to Do When Your Teen Is Underperforming Academically

The most common problem that parents of freshmen face is a "bad" report card after the first marking period. Parents wonder, "How could this have happened?"

They had asked their teen how things were going at school almost every day, and the answer was always the same, "Everything is fine." Now the report card is issued, and the results indicate that everything is certainly *not* fine! If you find you are in this situation, don't panic! You need to know a few things, and then a series of steps you will need to take to get your teen back on track.

HOW IMPORTANT ARE GRADES, ANYWAY?

It is hard to convince parents not to get too concerned over the first grading report of the year. However, it is important to know that these initial grades are really designed to serve as a communication tool. They are a way for the teachers to let the parent know what the student's learning levels are at that time. Parents should look at these grades as "progress" reports. Often, we've had to reassure parents, explaining that the only grades that really matter are the "final" grades at the end of the semester and year. In the long term, these are the only grades that college admissions officers will ever see. These grades are, indeed, very important to your student's future, but it's important that you don't overreact to a bad initial report card. We counsel you to take it as it is intended to be taken: As an indication of how your student is doing early in the school year. If you determine that your student is underperforming, then simply follow the steps we outline in this chapter. First, however, you need to understand how your kid's grades got so bad in the first place.

How Do Teachers Calculate Grades?

This is a good question to have asked before you reached this point! Many students and parents learn this the hard way, however. A great rule of thumb is to learn, as quickly as possible from the beginning of any class, is how each teacher calculates his or her grades. It's called "playing the grade game". Our most successful students are very systematic about achieving the grades they want. They figure out very early what types of assignments "count" most in class, and they make sure that they always perform well on those items. We know what you're thinking: "Don't all teachers grade the same? I thought there was one district-wide grading scale." Even if this statement is true, the way that teachers calculate grades can and will vary widely from teacher to teacher. Some teachers put a high value on class participation. Others care most about how a student performs on tests and quizzes. Others might put more weight on homework completion. Savvy students and parents will discover what their teachers' value the most and will do whatever is necessary to meet those expectations.

> *Insider's Tip: Almost every teacher has a unique way of calculating grades. Find out each of teacher's grading practices early in the year.*

Don't Let It Get This Far!

We know it's really not fair to say this to you, but we told you so! You need to actively monitor the progress of your student (Chapter 7) to ensure that you are on top of the academic progress before things get too out of hand! Maintain appropriate contact with your student's teachers to find out how things are going. Log in to your school's online parent information system to see the latest test and quiz grades your teen has earned. Make periodic spot checks of your student's daily planner to ensure they are carefully keeping track of the daily and long-range assignments and projects due for his or her classes. By sticking to this program, you will avoid the shock of seeing a poor report card in the first place.

MEET WITH YOUR STUDENT'S TEACHERS

Face-to-face meetings with your teen's teachers are invaluable when your student is struggling. Phone conversations and emails work fine when things are going well, but there is no substitute for a face-to-face meeting when things aren't going so well. In our experience, sitting down with your student and his or her teacher is the quickest and most effective way to find positive solutions to whatever it is that is causing your teen to struggle in class. As school insiders, however, we see many of these meeting go astray and fail to achieve their purpose. Therefore, we are going to offer you these basic guidelines for having a pleasant and beneficial meeting with your student's teachers:

- **Don't accept no for an answer! (but be accommodating).** Your child's teachers are busy people. They will often try to avoid having a face-to-face meeting in lieu of a phone conversation or an email. Don't let this happen, but remember you are asking them for extra time and effort. Set the meeting when it is most convenient for the teacher, whether before or after school, or even in the middle of the school day during their planning period. Teachers are rarely afforded this courtesy, and it will set things off on the right foot right from the start.
- **Be sure that your student attends the meeting!** We can't tell you how often we've seen parent-teacher conferences taking place without the student involved. This situation is crazy! High school is all about the student taking more responsibility for his own learning. If the parent and the teacher are going to take the time to try to address why the student is underperforming in class, then the student should be involved in the discussion.

After all, it is the student who will need to make the necessary adjustments to avoid being in this same situation again at the end of the next grading period.

- **Don't try to place blame for your student's poor grades.** If your goal is to come to the meeting to blame the teacher for the bad grades, whether because of poor instruction or faulty assessment, don't waste your time with this meeting. (See Chapter 10, "My kid's teacher stinks!") The only thing you'll achieve is to put your student's teacher on the defensive and make the problem worse. Come to the meeting to find out what your student can do to remediate or relearn what was missed during the past grading period. Also, find out how you can help your student avoid getting into this same situation during the subsequent grading periods.

- **Focus on learning rather than on grades.** Teachers hate to hear, "What can my kid do to pull up this grade?" This question is really asking the teacher to come up with some extra-credit, which translates to the teacher as "more work for me!" Try to focus the meeting on learning goals. What did the student fail to learn during the marking period? What specific assignments and grading factors caused the low grade (i.e., low test grades, missing projects, etc.). These types of questions are music to teachers' ears. Once you frame the meeting in this way, it is much more likely that the teacher will be amenable to helping your student get back on track.

- **Formalize the plan that you develop in the meeting.** We often hear parents come out of these conferences with vague and unformed plans like, "So my kid can come and see you after school for more help?" As school insiders, we have seen many such well-intentioned plans end unsuccessfully. What we'd like to see is the student, teacher, and parent all to know exactly what, when, and how the student will address the academic shortcomings. For instance, a plan such as, "My son will be in your room at 3:15 every Tuesday and Thursday until you send me a note letting me know he is back on track" is preferable. We have seen positive results come out of an "academic contract" developed at the meeting where each person's responsibility is clearly articulated, and each person signs to show agreement with the terms of the contract.

- **Take the time to write your teacher a note reviewing the outcomes of the meeting and** *thank them!* We recommend a follow up to these meetings that summarizes what was achieved. Remember, high school teachers will often have more than 150 students. At the end of the grading period, your meeting with them will not be the only parent/teacher/student conference they attended that week. By reviewing and clarifying your understanding of the outcomes of the meeting, you have once again put your student's interests in the forefront of the teacher's mind. Also, you'd be surprised to know how infrequently teachers are thanked for their time and efforts. Write a sincere thank-you note letting them know how impressed you were with their professionalism and how confident you are that, together, you'll be able to help your child get up to speed in the class. Then, if you really want to make the teacher happy, send a short note to the principal letting him or her know how incredibly helpful and professional the teacher was in the meeting. Principals love to receive these types of notes and are sure to give the teacher accolades when they receive one. Teachers always appreciate it and are more likely to go out of their way to help your student succeed, and to reach back out to you should anything go wrong in the future

FIND THE RESOURCES AVAILABLE TO HELP YOUR STUDENT

High schools are offering a more varied and complicated curriculum to students. A time will come when parents will look at the schoolwork their teen is doing and will think, "I can't do that!" So, how can parents expect to be able to help their kid when he is struggling in a class? Well, there is good news. Since the No Child Left Behind Act of

2001, schools are judged by how well their students perform on "high stakes" tests. As a result, students have more resources than ever to help them recover when they are struggling in their academics. It is usually only the savvy parents, however, who are aware of these resources and know how to help their students tap into them. A visit to your school's counseling department will inform you of all of these opportunities for help. You are likely to find resources such as:

- **Scheduled tutorials.** Many schools have begun to build "tutorial" periods into their regular school day. These tutorials can be either mandatory or voluntary and serve as a way for students to have small group or individual instruction with their teachers. We suggest that you coach your student to approach his or her teachers with specific requests for instruction (such as, "I don't really understand how to solve this equation for X. Can you explain it to me again?"), rather than simply showing up and saying, "What should I do?" or "I'm lost."

- **Peer tutoring.** Schools often enlist the help of their top students to work with students who are struggling. Often groups such as the National Honor Society do this regularly as part of their service requirements. Research shows that this student-to-student direct help is one of the most effective means of remediating students who are behind in academic classes. Ask your school's counseling department when tutorial groups hold tutorial sessions. If there is no existing program, ask the sponsor if a National Honor Society member might be found who would be interested in offering their help. Sometimes the sponsor will have a list of students who are willing to do peer tutoring as needed.

- **Private tutoring.** Schools will often have lists of private adult tutors who offer their services to do one-on-one remedial instruction for students who are struggling in class. These tutors typically charge $25 to $50 per hour for this service. Online tutorial services are also available for much less.

- **Remedial software programs.** Some schools have purchased software and loaded it in computer labs to give additional

Lorraine Swanson

Study groups such as this often result in a better understanding of course material and are good practice for future learning at the collegiate level.

instructional opportunities for students who have demonstrated they are behind in core academic areas. These lab opportunities are usually after-school programs. If your school does not offer these, you can often purchase individual licenses for these programs for your home computer.

- **Homework clubs.** Some schools organize "homework clubs" where struggling students are supported in completing their homework before they leave school for the day. These programs are usually offered after school. If your student's grades are low due to "zeroes" from not handing in work, these programs are especially effective.
- **Study groups.** Some parents have found success by asking their student's teacher to recommend one or more "study buddies" to work with their teen. This practice is one that will certainly benefit any student who will be going to a college or university, as study groups are a popular way for college students to stay on top of the strenuous workload expected in

many post-secondary institutions.

- **When all else fails, Google™ it!** We have had parents tell us they have found free and useful help on various internet sites. Video tutorials can be accessed on sites such as YouTube™ or TeacherTube™ for any number of topics and subjects.

Sometimes, as we write these chapters, we tend to make it all sound easy. It isn't. Once you have done what we suggested, you will find that the day-to-day follow-through of the plan can be a long and laborious task. What is most important, however, is that you stick to it. The worst message you can send to your teen is that you are going to give up when the plan you helped forge gets rough. Send the message that getting out of a hole like this isn't easy; but with your help, they can do it.

A time may come when you will have to put your foot down and tell your teen that they can't go to the Friday football game, or to the school dance, or to the movies because they failed to live up to the agreement made with you and the teachers. Although hard at the time, these lessons will pay huge dividends later in their high school career. Don't waffle on this! You'll be glad later that you stuck to your plan and helped your teen get back on track for success in high school. We promise.

Chapter Nine

My Kid's Teacher Stinks!
What to Do When You Think Your Teen's Teacher Is Ineffective

The vast majority of teachers your teen will encounter in high school are hard-working professionals who genuinely care about their students. However, there is, in almost every high school in America, a teacher or two who are not effective educators. Chances are the school administration is well aware of these teachers and, most likely, are already taking steps to fix the problem. Unfortunately, removing non-effective tenured teachers from the classroom is a difficult and time-consuming process. Often, this process takes up to two years or even longer to complete. In this chapter, we hope to help you figure out if your child has one of these teachers, and if so, what steps you can take to minimize the negative impact this teacher can have on your teen.

Before we venture into the problem of the really "bad" teacher, let's talk about a more common issue. Parents are often concerned about whether their teen's teachers are a "bad fit" for their child. In other words, they either believe there is a personality conflict between the student and teacher or their teen's learning style does not match the teacher's way of conducting the class. These situations are a bit more complicated and require some additional decisions on your part.

LET'S PUT "STINKS" IN PERSPECTIVE

As a parent of a ninth grade student, you will be working with your teen's principal for the next four years. If you begin these four years by showing up the first week of school demanding to have your child's schedule changed because of your immediate perception that your teen's teacher is incompetent, it will not set the stage for best meeting your child's needs. Our first piece of advice is for you to remain calm. Don't overreact based on some initial, anecdotal stories your teen tells you one evening about how a certain teacher "stinks."

> *Insider's Tip: "If you love your child, you will not speak negatively about teachers in front of them."*
> *—Dr. Freeman Hrabowski*

Let's put "stinks" in perspective. If your teen takes seven classes each year, they are likely to have 28 different high school teachers over the course of their career. There is a good chance that one or more will not be a perfect fit with your teen. Some may be too demanding. Some may not have a great personality and be all business. Some may be too strict. If you, as a parent, take a negative stance in the first month of the school year, the principal's reaction may not be sympathetic. There may be an occasion during the four years when your child does have a serious conflict with a teacher. So, as insiders, we are advising you to decide judiciously when it's time to walk into the school and request a teacher change.

If, and when, you decide it's absolutely critical to approach the principal about an ineffective teacher, this chapter will define the steps to take that will maximize your chances of success. Our suggestions will help you make the situation more positive and will make you look like the caring, supportive parent you are. If necessary, following our advice puts you in the best position to achieve a teacher change.

High School Teachers Are Different

Teachers do not "stink" because they raise their voice at your teen or because they may give challenging assignments. Teachers do not "stink" because your child does not feel comfortable talking with friends in class. The teacher who "stinks" is the one who does not instructionally challenge a child and does not care about the academic success of students. It is important to make this distinction and understand that not every high school teacher seems "caring," smiles at their students, and is as nurturing as your child's middle or elementary school teachers. Providing meaningful instruction to high school students, promoting effective classroom discipline, and ensuring a good learning environment often requires teachers to have a sterner, more direct approach than some freshmen are used to experiencing in school.

In fact, some of the best high school teachers come across as "gruff" at first. Principals are used to having parents complain about teachers such as these in the first few weeks of a school year. However, principals also know which teachers have the greatest positive influence on students, and believe it or not, these teachers are often one in the same. We can't tell

Although no parent wants to ever see their child become disengaged in a class, the hardest thing is figuring out if you should do something about it.

you how many times former students have come back after a year in college to relate how they now respect and appreciate the teachers who were the toughest on them in high school. They often now hold the teachers they did not like or appreciate in extremely high regard. It is the rare student who really appreciates teachers who require their students to work hard, be responsible, and reach their potential while in high school.

The converse is also true. Alumni tell us that the "easy," often popular, high school teachers did not prepare them for their futures. An excellent, effective teacher has the skills to balance both the rigor appropriate for a high school classroom and the compassion needed to maximize instruction and excite teenagers to learn.

Sometimes It's Okay to Let Your Child "Build Character"

Don't be in a rush to solve every conflict your teen has with their high school teachers. These struggles may, in fact, be beneficial to the overall development of your child. In previous generations, students were expected to deal with problems such as managing a demanding teacher. These experiences helped to "build character." This conclusion still holds true, but we recognize that there is a fine line between "building character" and jeopardizing your teen's future by not taking action as a parent.

Teaching is much like many other professions. There are a few really great teachers, a good number of solid, effective teachers, another large group of average teachers, and, unfortunately, a few really ineffective teachers. We know of no profession in the world where this pattern does not hold true. Think about it for a second. It's true with doctors, lawyers, professional athletes, world leaders, writers, and really, any profession.

We wish every teacher could be a superstar. Certainly, superstars generate a lot of positive, public accolades for schools. However, the measure of a school often lies in how effective teachers are as a whole group. Every school has some superstars, but the great schools make all their teachers feel like superstars.

It is a beneficial life lesson for your teenager to realize that being a successful person often means adapting yourself to fit the nuances of your teacher, your professor, your boss, or your customer. In fact, adjusting to different teachers is a necessary skill to develop for future success. Surmounting these struggles makes students stronger and indeed will help them "build the character" traits they will rely on to achieve future successes in the workplace as well.

So How Do You Know When the Teacher Really "Stinks"

For a minute, think back to your high school teachers. Did you have a really bad one? No matter how bad the experience was, how much damage did the bad teacher really do in the long run? The answer is probably, "little or none." When a teen complains about his or her teacher, keep this question in mind: Is the teacher so ineffective that their practice will jeopardize your child's future? We can tell you stories of our high school days and recount a poor teacher or two. At the time, it caused some frustrations, but in perspective, looking back on our educations, these teachers had little lasting impact. In fact, these poor teachers may have motivated us to work harder as teachers and educators! Stronger students are impacted less by one bad teacher. Strong students often succeed despite a bad teacher. These students are so driven that they don't let ineffective teachers stand in their way. However, the needier a student, the greater the negative impact can be from a teacher who can't interest a student in learning.

Most principals will tell you they can recognize a problem with a teacher based on frequent observations in the classroom. If the students are engaged in meaningful instruction based on the curriculum, that teacher is doing a fine job. If students are bored, have their heads on the desks, are frequently disruptive and exhibit an obvious lack of focus or interest in the instruction taking place in the room, there is a problem.

As a parent, there are some key factors you should look for when making a determination about your teen's teachers. First, is the class a core class or an "elective" or non-core class? For example, an ineffective English or math teacher might have a larger negative impact on your teen than an unsatisfactory ninth grade physical education teacher. Secondly, listen exactly to what your child is saying about the teacher. If the complaints center on tough expectations, difficult assignments, or not being "nice," then these complaints might warrant a discussion or a conference with the teacher, but not a demand for a teacher change. In fact, some of these complaints by your teen may actually be good for successful learning in the long run.

If your teen's complaints, however, center on things like the classroom being chaotic or unruly, feeling nervous or afraid in class, or having no idea what is supposed to be learned in the classroom, you might have a legitimate reason to be concerned. If your child tells you that the teacher is "not teaching us anything" or that the teacher won't answer questions when your teen is confused, a red flag should go up. If your child tells you students are bored and never have any work to do for the class, then again you may have a good reason for concern.

What the Principal Is Thinking

The first thing to remember is that if you are dealing with a really inef-fective teacher, the principal likely already knows there is a problem. Unless you are dealing with a brand new teacher, chances are the prin-cipal has received similar complaints from other parents regarding the teacher. The principal also knows instinctively if you are overreacting. For example, there may be some teachers who routinely receive criti-cisms at the beginning of year, but by the end of the year, those same teachers win praise from their students and parents. Your complaint against a specific teacher may be the only one received regarding that teacher. This complaint might inform the principal that the issue is between the student and the teacher and things will work out through a conference or mediation. In other words, the principal has "histori-cal" knowledge about the teacher. As a parent, you should trust the administrators' professionalism and listen to their recommendations when you have a concern.

The principal must look at problems and issues from both an individual child's perspective and from a larger perspective of how an intervention might impact the entire school. The default reaction may be to deny a request for a teacher change. Parents sometimes will get frustrated at this decision because the principal will not quickly switch their teen out of a specific teacher's class simply because the parents are requesting the change. The school principal is looking at the domino effect of such a decision. If the principal allows your child to switch to a new teacher's class, how many other parents might come forward requesting a change? A high school master schedule is a complex instrument and, quite honestly, switching students freely from teacher to teacher wreaks havoc. This action results in classes being unbal-anced and sets a dangerous school–wide precedent. A prudent princi-pal will always try to solve the problem between the student and the teacher, rather than quickly agree to make an alternate teacher assign-ment. So, for the principal, the default answer to a request for a teacher change will usually be, "No." The goal is to solve the teacher/student conflict and continue the year successfully with the student remaining in the original teacher's classroom. So, as a parent, you need to be prepared for this initial reaction.

Insider's Tip: Savvy parents get the principal on their side. When they need help or consideration, the principal becomes a valuable advocate for their teen.

HOW TO GET YOUR CHILD'S TEACHER CHANGED

Keeping in mind everything we have discussed in this chapter about not overreacting to the teacher issue, we agree that some situations warrant a schedule change. Here are some strategies that will greatly enhance your chances of success when requesting a teacher change. Keep in mind that getting a student's teacher changed is a delicate and difficult task. Even if you follow all our strategies, there is no guarantee that your request will be successful. However, we believe our advice puts you in the best position possible to make the change happen.

The most important thing to remember is that you want to work with the principal. You want to create an atmosphere of cooperation, being open to suggestions from the principal rather than creating resentment by making negative attacks on the school or teacher. Remember, the goal is your student's success.

The Proactive Approach

Changing a schedule before the school year starts is easier than changing the schedule after school is in session. Often, a proactive approach with the administration will help diffuse potential problems. If you have legitimate concerns about your child receiving a certain teacher, approach the principal with this concern before the school year begins. Sometimes a student or the student's sibling has been in the teacher's class before, and either failed or was miserable for the entire year. For example, we have had parents write letters to us well in advance of the school year indicating that, even though they know we don't honor specific teacher requests, they request that their student not be placed with a certain teacher based on past experience. When a principal reads this letter, steps will often be taken to ensure that the child is placed in a different teacher's class simply to avoid having to deal with this issue later in the year.

Principals can read between the lines of a request letter like the one we describe. Simply put, a principal will realize that the placement of your teen in this particular teacher's classroom will result in any number of problems during the course of the year, problems that will directly impact the principal's work load. If these problems can be easily avoided by simply making the change before the school year begins, it is likely to happen. This is a good strategy if you have a feeling there might be a problem even before schedules are distributed. A word of warning: You can only use this approach once, or maybe twice at most, over an entire high school career.

Sometimes, parents are actually using this strategy to get their child into a preferred teacher's class, rather than out of an unwanted teacher's class. Parents use this strategy usually because there is one teacher who is perceived as a "better" option. If you are trying this strategy, you can be sure that half of the parents in your teen's class are doing the same. Bottom line, the principal will see right through this ploy, and it will probably not work. This approach is more successful when you are using it to avoid having your student enrolled in a particular teacher's class rather than getting your child into a class with any specific teacher.

The Conference Approach

If you have valid concerns, request a conference with the teacher and ask that either the guidance counselor and/or the assistant principal attend. Do not schedule this conference before you have heard what the teacher says at Back to School Night. In most high schools, Back to School Night is not designed for individual conferences with teachers, but you can gain some valuable information from the teacher's presentation to you. You can use this information to evaluate your child's complaints about the teacher. If your concerns are still strong, schedule a conference. You do not have to wait until the first grading period is over.

With your teen in attendance, you should clearly state your concerns. It is not conducive to success to make personal attacks on the teacher. It is more effective to take a business-like approach, sharing your concern in an open manner in the hopes of finding a way to help your child experience improved learning. Keep an open mind. You may find that many of your conceptions were a result of bad or biased information from your teen. Be open to compromise with the teacher and allow the teacher to present his or her perspective on your concerns. This conference should end in a collaborative plan of action for the success of your teen. We would also encourage a timetable for a follow-up meeting to review the action plan and decide on the next steps to be taken.

After this conference one of three things is going to happen. One possibility is that things will improve and your concerns will be alleviated. You should still have the follow-up meeting with the teacher and others attending the initial conference to address further concerns that may arise from either side.

The second possibility is that the conference is a disaster. In our years as school principals this situation happens only rarely, but it does happen. Usually when the conference has been a disaster, the teacher becomes flustered and may be unwilling to develop a plan to meet the needs of your teen. If this happens, remain calm and professional because your position has just been greatly strengthened. If there is an assistant principal or guidance counselor attending the conference, request that the principal be informed of the outcomes of the meeting. Document your concerns and the attitude of the teacher. If there is resistance, contact the principal yourself. It may be that you will need to attend another meeting with a counselor or administrator, but it is now likely that your wishes for a schedule change will be honored. The school may simply want to end this ugly situation.

Insiders Tip: When requesting a teacher change, make the request in writing directly to the Principal. He or she may delegate the action to an Assistant Principal, but remains aware of your concerns. However, be sure that you do not put the request in writing before trying to take some steps to solve the situation first.

The third possibility is that the conference goes well. A plan is developed, but in reality nothing improves in the classroom. If this situation occurs, then you need to make a critical decision.

First, contact the principal and make an official request in writing (either attached to an email or hand delivered) to schedule another conference. Approach the conversation with the principal in a strategic way. First, make sure the principal knows that you are not angry, but rather are looking for help. You might say things like, "I appreciate your time and effort in helping to solve this problem. I'm really frustrated by this process because my child is struggling, and we've tried to work it out with the teacher without success. Now we need your help."

Insiders Note: When you are dealing with the Principal on important issues like a teacher reassignment, always do it in a face-to-face meeting. Email and/or phone conversations will decrease your chance of getting a favorable intervention.

Be as specific as possible about your concerns and frustrations with the principal. Avoid getting overly emotional. Detail the work you have done to try to make the situation a better one and be prepared to demonstrate how the teacher has not lived up to the plan everyone had agreed to previously. Share your opinions on why this teacher is not cooperating to solve the problem, but be factual. Discuss only what relates to your teen; do not gossip or talk about hearsay. Remember, the principal has to be able to justify why your situation is special to make a teacher change. Do your part by giving the factual details needed to make a favorable decision.

One last piece of advice: If you get your way, don't talk about it in the community. A principal who sided with you against one of the teachers is risking having made an unpopular decision with the staff. If the principal finds out that a parent has spread word of this "victory" in public, you can be sure that you will never be on the receiving end of a close decision again. Protect your own interests by protecting the principal. Keep quiet about this issue and direct your teen to both keep quiet about this decision and to stay respectful toward the former teacher.

The Squeaky Wheel Approach

First, we should warn you about using this approach. As principals, we can positively say we hate it when parents become squeaky wheels. However, we recognize that this approach does work sometimes, and therefore as school insiders trying to give you an inside edge, we have decided to share it. However, be warned that if you choose to use this approach, you will likely damage the positive relationships we have encouraged you to develop with school personnel.

The squeaky wheel approach is exactly what it purports to be. This approach is the parent who continues to call, email, write, pester, and intercept administrators in the hallway to complain about the teacher in question. In fact, this approach tends to get results (albeit begrudgingly).

While it is true that some "squeaky wheel" parents who show up at school unannounced and demand to meet with the principal sometimes get their way, we don't recommend this approach. It is far more diplomatic to call in advance and request a meeting. Otherwise, you may have to wait for a while or come back another day if the principal is out of the building at a meeting. Principals are always willing to meet with parents when it has been properly requested and scheduled.

The real squeaky parents don't stop with the principal. They keep going all the way to the superintendent and School Board if they have to. As stated before, the positive relationships you have made with school personnel can (and will most likely) be damaged, but sometimes this technique gets results. Whatever the issue, make sure it is extremely important to you because even if the squeaky wheel gets the grease at that time, it doesn't mean that the principal is going to forget about how you achieved your goal when you have future problems.

Chapter Ten

My Kid's Friends Stink!

What to Do When You Think Your Teen's Friends
Are Bad Influences

One of the often overlooked factors in a student's success is the peer group that the student is associated with in high school. A high school principal once told us about an interaction with a parent who attempted to provide his children the best chances for developing a positive peer group. The story this principal recounts follows:

One spring afternoon, a dad I had never met before approached me as we were preparing to dismiss students from school. He introduced himself as a newcomer to our community and informed me that his children would arrive in the summer and would enroll as students the following school year. Then he asked what I thought, at first, was an odd question. He asked, "What activity or sport should I encourage my children to participate in?" I really didn't know what to answer, so I asked what his children's interests were. He replied, "That doesn't really matter since I want my kids to associate with the best kids in the school." Immediately, I realized what a great question he asked! I answered, "You want them to run cross-country. At this school, the coach is amazing, the kids are supportive and friendly, and they are all on the honor roll." He smiled and said, "Thank you." I had forgotten all about this interaction until the next fall when I saw this parent at a cross-country meet, and he thanked me for the great advice I gave him. His children had transitioned to our school smoothly, they had made great friends, their grades were excellent, and they were happy with their new home.

Upon reflection, we realize just how savvy this dad was. He knew that a key factor in his kids' transition to this new school and community would be surrounding his children with other successful kids.

This story leads to our first piece of advice for you regarding your teen's social life. As parents, you must do everything you can do to minimize the chances that your teen will make bad decisions in forming a new social network. You can accomplish this by ensuring that your student is scheduled in college preparatory courses and is involved in sports, clubs, and activities that have a reputation for excellence in your school. This approach is not foolproof, but you are increasing the odds that your teen will find great new friends with whom to experience high school.

As school insiders, who have dealt with more than our fair share of kids who have made bad choices and were forced to deal with the consequences, we can tell you that the majority of students whom we deal with administratively get into these situations by following the bad advice of one of their friends. Whether it is cutting class, smoking in the restroom, bullying another student, or something much worse, there is usually a ringleader and several followers. Invariably, parents say to us, "We knew that kid was trouble!" When that happens, we, of course, are thinking, "Then why did you let your kid hang around with him!" But we know it's not that easy. In fact, helping your teen select appropriate friends is a hard thing to accomplish.

As your teen enters high school, it is quite natural for a teenager to "branch out" and expand their social circle. As your child begins to embrace new interests, clubs, and sports, it is natural to come into contact with students and make new friends whom you have never met and know nothing about. As they begin to identify who they are as individuals, you may find that they are interested in spending less and less time with kids with whom you are acquainted. In short, they are growing up and changing, and as this happens, their social groups may shift and change.

There is nothing wrong with this natural progression of having new, different, and varied friends, but you must certainly stay aware. Many unwise decisions can be made when a teen is trying to "win

Corepics

Students will often develop new peer groups as they enter high school. Every parent's nightmare is that their teen begins to mix with a "bad crowd".

over" or impress the members of this new social set. The best case scenario (and this happens quite frequently) is that your child's new friends will have a positive and beneficial influence on them. These new relationships will hopefully result in the healthy development of your child, and the whole experience of an expanding social circle will be enriching and enjoyable for both you and your teen. On the other hand, it is possible that your teenager will choose to hang around with those who will be bad influences.

> *Insider's Tip: The classes your student is scheduled for can have a huge impact on which social circle they gravitate towards. If you want your student to be surrounded with friends who have similar goals and aspirations, be sure they are scheduled into the most rigorous academic classes appropriate for their ability.*

At this point, it is important for us to share some things we've observed about ninth grade students that will help you understand why a teen is making the social decisions a teenager makes. Most of the time, students will fall into these patterns:

- Ninth grade boys are struggling between wanting to still behave as a kid (playing war in the woods, playing with action figures, and just being goofy) and wanting to become a "man." When he is associating with the friends you know, he will often behave exactly as he did when he was in middle school. When you see him with a new group, you will see your son acting very differently. He may even look, talk, and behave as if he were a complete stranger. You'll be thinking, "Who is this kid?" Unfortunately, sometimes a new circle of friends will influence a ninth grade boy to experiment in behaviors that he has not been exposed to before. A ninth grade boy will be pressured to take part in some of these things or risk alienation by this new circle.
- Ninth grade girls are generally more mature than their male counterparts. They will often be tempted to hang out with the "older" crowd. Ninth grade girls are more likely to be invited to attend social functions (homecoming dances, proms) and parties with junior and senior boys. Once your teen is in a situation with older students, the likelihood of her feeling pressured to make risky decisions increases dramatically. This pressure is a huge deal for ninth grade girls because they can become highly conflicted about making good decisions, but risk "everyone" not liking them because they choose not to participate in certain activities. If your instincts tell you that your daughter is being put into these situations, trust these feelings. She will likely get upset, but you know there will be plenty of time for her to participate in the activities designed for older children when she is in those grades. Don't let her be in a rush to grow up.
- In both cases, being asked to join these new social circles is fun and exciting for your teen. They want to feel cool and be accepted as part of their new group. This is normal and healthy,

but it is when they are just getting to know these new friends that they are likely to try new things, things that are risky. In order to fit it, your teen might find it difficult to resist engaging in certain behaviors (shoplifting, cutting school, vandalism, drinking, smoking, doing drugs, sexual activity, etc.) that you would be shocked they would even consider. This is the time for you to be on high alert. As a parent, you must be in tune with the constant severe pressure many ninth graders deal with when trying to "fit in" with a new social group of friends.

We suggest that you keep a close watch as they begin to branch out into these new groups. We counsel parents to:

- **Look for changes in behavior, dress, and language.** Many times, changing social groups will quickly impact the way your teen dresses, behaves, and communicates. These often benign changes are of little consequence, but we think it is important that you let your teen know that you noticed the difference. There is a fine line between innocent changes (hair style, clothing choices, and/or music preferences) and more telltale warning signs (piercings, tattoos, dramatic hairstyle changes, wholesale clothing changes, or even certain music). Don't make fun of, or belittle, the changes, but ask about them and show interest. As school insiders, we have observed time and again that changes in behavior, dress, and language frequently accompany the adoption of new bad habits, such as smoking marijuana. Stay alert for warning signs.
- **Pay attention to academic issues.** As students are transitioning to a new social group, everything else may become secondary in importance to this new and exciting development. It is your job to help your teen keep their "eyes on the prize" and maintain a good academic standing.
- **Develop rapport with your child's new friends and make an effort to contact their parents.** In middle school, you were likely to have known your child's friends for many years. If your

teen develops new friends in high school, make an effort to get to know these kids (and the parents) as well. Offer to drive your child's new group to a school function or to a social event. Talk to your child's friends. Get to know them, their interests, goals and their backgrounds. You might see some eye-rolling from your teen, but everyone will know you are interested and involved in your teen's life. Also, try to make contact with your teen's new friend's parents, especially if they begin to spend time together outside of school. This way both your teen and their new friends know that all the adults in their lives are watching, a good message to send to teenagers.

- **Make sure you know where your child is, why they are there, and who they are with.** We are amazed when we find out that parents will allow their teen to "go out" on weekends with their friends without knowing where they are going, what they are doing, or whom they are with. For example, if your child says, "We are going to hang out at Cameron's house," it is a good idea for you to ask, "Cameron who? What is his phone number? What are you going to do there? Are his parents going to be home?" If those questions are easily answered, call Cameron's parents and exchange phone numbers. This technique is especially important when your teen is engaging with new social groups and sends a clear message to your son or daughter, their new friends, and their new friend's parents, that you care about your teen's well-being and are actively monitoring what he or she is doing.

If you follow these basic steps, your instincts will help you make informed decisions about your teen's new friends. Most of the time, you will find these new acquaintances to be nice, friendly, positive children who you are happy to have around your family members. Other times, however, you will develop an uneasy feeling and will feel that it may be necessary to intervene between your teen and this new group. If this situation is the case, we recommend you do so carefully.

Insider's Tip: It is amazing how much you will learn by simply dialoguing with your teen and your teen's friends and being an "active" listener. Teens love to talk about their lives and the lives of their friends.

Potentially, the most difficult thing you control as a high school parent is impacting whom your teen chooses for friends. Your instincts may tell you that an association will result in negative consequences, from bad grades to getting into serious trouble, and you want your kid away from these "bad seeds" fast! Unfortunately, one of the easiest ways to alienate yourself from your teen is to criticize friends. Teenagers can be fiercely loyal to their friends, even those who are not good for them. If you develop some concerns regarding your teen and the choices being made regarding friends, consider some of the following advice to help deal with this delicate issue.

Our first piece of advice is to relax. Chances are that you have done a good job preparing your teen with the ability to recognize bad decisions and avoid them. You will not be able to shelter your teen from all the "bad influences" in life. This is the time to develop the ability to identify trouble, and stay away from it. Even if the friend really is a bad influence, your child may recognize that influence sooner or later, and what you will notice is that the friendship you were worried about has run its course without any interference from you at all.

A good rule of thumb for parents faced with this problem is:

- **Calmly and rationally discuss your concerns with your child.** Try to stay unemotional about the issue you are presenting. Discuss the changes in your teen that have become evident since the exposure to these new friends. Avoid being overly critical of your child's new friends; instead, focus on specific actions, behaviors, and issues you find worrisome.
- **Review your child's goals and vision for the future.** Discuss whether these new friends are going to help or hinder your

teen's ultimate goals and dreams. Explain that you aren't trying to shut your child off from branching out, but you are trying to keep them focused on the future and you're worried that their actions are not supporting your child reaching their potential as a student or a person.

- **Talk to your child's school administrator and counselor.** Sometimes it may be possible for you to enlist the support and guidance of school officials in helping you get your message across to your teen. Dialogue with the school counselor and teachers to see if they are seeing some of the same troubling behavior and attitudes you are seeing. It may be possible to change your student's schedule to separate your child from these negative influences.

- **Tell your child that, "They are *not* all doing it."** High school students are very susceptible to believing that "everyone is doing it," including staying out late, smoking pot, cheating on tests, getting drunk, or having sex. Sociologists call this the "social norms theory," and it is dangerous. Once students believe that "everyone is doing it," they are much more likely to engage in that behavior because they figure they will do it eventually anyway. No matter what "it" is, everyone is *not* doing it. Just because some in your teen's social circle are engaging in a risky behavior does not mean that it is the norm. This is just the perception. Even if the majority of kids ARE doing it, that doesn't mean your kid has to do it too! Remind your teen that it is okay to "just say no." If those friends don't like that, or won't accept your teen with that stance, then most teenagers will realize they aren't very good friends anyway.

- **Let your child use you as an excuse.** Many times parents have told us that their children were relieved when they confronted them on these issues. The children said that, once they entered this new group, they didn't see any way they could get away. Once their parents confronted them on this issue, they told their children, "Use us as an excuse if you need to." This strategy was just what the student was looking for. They simply told the other kids, "I'm not allowed to come over here anymore. My Dad is such a jerk!" and that solved the problem.

Even if your teen is resentful at first when you intervene, if you provide a rational explanation of why you are concerned, your child will usually appreciate that you took a strong and authoritative stand. Students know, even if it is subconsciously, that they are being too risky, and they appreciate when their parents put limits and boundaries on them.

Chapter Eleven

Uh-oh! It's the Principal!
What to Do When Your Teen Gets in Trouble

The phone call no parent likes to receive is when the principal or assistant principal calls home to say that your teen has gotten into trouble at school. As principals, we don't enjoy the phone calls either (contrary to the beliefs of some of our students!). After making hundreds of these types of calls, we have seen how savvy parents expertly react to these difficult circumstances. Unfortunately, we have also seen some parents at their worst when trying to deal with these situations. This chapter will outline how to deal with the "dreaded phone call." We will help you put these calls and your child's infractions into perspective. We will give you some ideas on how to appeal the decision made in those situations if you feel your teen wasn't treated fairly. Finally, we will outline some ways to handle yourself if your teen is involved in some extremely serious discipline infractions at school.

If you think that this chapter does not pertain to you because your child has never gotten into trouble, you might want to reconsider this stance. We have seen all sorts of students get into trouble at school. Some students are routine offenders who are really struggling in school. Sometimes, though, students that have had a great record before high school start to do things parents would consider out of character. Last, some of our best performing students in the school have made major mistakes at some point, even putting them in a position to be considered for expulsion. At the very least, we recommend that you give this chapter a quick read for reference. Keep it on your book shelf and use it if you ever receive one of these dreaded phone calls. Hopefully, you'll never have to use it, but have the confidence to know all our advice and step-by-step instructions are there for you should you need it.

THE CODE OF CONDUCT AND A HARD DISCUSSION

Every school division should have a document that is called something like the "Code of Conduct" or "Code of Behavior." This document has probably been coming home to you every year since kindergarten. You probably glanced at it the first time you saw it, thought it really didn't apply to your five-year-old, and never looked at it again. Suddenly, your five-year-old is now a fourteen-year-old and getting ready to go to high school. It is time to look at this document again and discuss it with your teen.

Even though your teenager might give you a deep sigh, roll his or her eyes, and look at you like you are crazy, if you are a savvy parent (and we know you are since you're reading this book), you will sit with your teen and have this discussion. First, read the "Code of Conduct" document. To begin the discussion, ask your child if the teacher went over the document in school. (The answer to this question should be "yes.") Next, ask about the things that can get a student in major trouble. If you get no response, prompt your child with the answers based on your review of the document. Now, every school division is different and everyone's rules vary slightly, but we are sure every school division has severe consequences for what we call the "big ticket items," usually violence, weapons, drugs and alcohol. These misbehaviors carry the most severe disciplinary consequences.

This part of the conversation with your teenager may be awkward and uncomfortable, but it will absolutely pay off in the long run. You must clearly state your expectations about what is acceptable in your house and in your family. You must clearly state that their education is too important to jeopardize over these types of infractions. Even if you believe your child would never get involved with these "big ticket items," you must still have this conversation. Unfortunately, every high school in America (both public and private) has to deal with these issues. So, even though you don't feel that your teen is likely to become involved, every student will most definitely be exposed to other children who are involved with these things. In fact, your children could have already witnessed other children doing these types of things in middle school.

> *Insider's Note: Research says that when a teenager is faced with a critical decision in life, that the influence of peers (both positive and negative) and the influence of parents and families make the difference in their actions.*

During this conversation, teens often act like you are pulling teeth right out of their mouths, or that you are so out of touch with reality that it is actually painful to be related to you. We're telling you don't be deterred. It's okay; many parents have been made to feel just like you. In fact, think about how you treated your parents when you were fourteen years old. The most important thing to remember is that even though teens act like they don't care and that they aren't listening, the research and our experience show that they are indeed hearing and internalizing what their parents are saying; and what their parents say makes a difference. Don't expect your teenager to jump up and say, "thank you" and give you a big hug. In fact, the dramatic finish to this discussion will go something like this: "Is that it?" or "Are we done?" or even, "Can I go now?"

When you finish this conversation (and really this whole discussion need not be more than 15 minutes), tell your teen that they are free to go if they can repeat back to you the main points of your discussion. Those main points should be those few things that will get a student into serious trouble at school. Your teen needs to be able to tell you what your family's expectations are about those things. As the discussion concludes, convey to your teen that this chat was held because you care and love them.

> *Insider's Note: Children (at any age) need boundaries. When you discuss difficult topics with them, they appreciate knowing the rules and your expectations. It's one more way in which you show your children how much you care about them.*

MINOR TROUBLE

Let's say that you get a call from the school administrator that your teen received a discipline referral because of something that you might deem minor. By minor, we really mean something of small consequence. Consequences for minor referrals might include a warning, a conference, counseling, a detention, or even a Saturday detention.

Many times when this call is made, parents have one of two initial reactions. They either want to scream and yell at their child, or they want to scream and yell at the school. Neither one is a good reaction. Again, we think it's easy to say in a book, and we admit that we have received such a call from the school about our own children and our first reaction was one of the two above.

When we were young, we clearly remember that one strategy our parents would use was to send us to our rooms and not discuss the incident. As children we hated this because we did not know what our parents were going to do (the fear of the unknown). As adults, we realize our parents were simply buying some time so they could think about the situation and deal with it in a logical rather than an emotional way.

MY CHILD SAYS HE DIDN'T DO IT

Anytime your teen receives a disciplinary consequence, the school should provide you with a clear explanation of what happened and why your child was punished. Your teen may give you a different version of what happened. So, what do you do?

First, ask yourself this question, "What would my parents have done?" If your parents were like ours, there probably wasn't much of a discussion. The default answer in our homes was: The school was right, the teacher was right, or the principal was right. Although our parents may have not really believed these statements, they never voiced any disagreement in front of us as teenagers. They may have had these types of discussions between themselves, but ultimately realized that you don't have to fight every battle.

Second, keep it in perspective. If the consequences are minor, you need to consider whether this issue is worth fighting the battle. Think about the message that appealing a minor issue sends to the school and your child. Is this going to hurt your child in the long run? Will it put their future in jeopardy? Quite honestly, there is nothing wrong with letting a teen "deal with it." In other words, it's okay for your child to know that you as the parent are not going to ride in on a white horse and save the day for every minor thing they are dealing with in life.

We'd like you to look at the situation from a principal's perspective. When the principal receives your appeal (along with hundreds of daily emails, phone calls, and stacks of paperwork), they are likely to think, "Are you kidding me? Is this parent really appealing such a minor thing?" What you have really done is added hours of work to your principal's day. The principal must now relook or reinvestigate the situation, make a decision (that will most likely upset someone, either the parent or the school's staff members/teachers), and respond to you formally in writing.

Of course, you may be saying to yourself, "That's what the principal gets paid to do." Let's consider that thought. A principal is responsible for dealing with budget issues, curriculum issues, and ensuring there are quality teachers in the classrooms. Sometimes, the principal deals with serious discipline infractions that might impact the overall safety of the entire school. Would you rather the principal take time away from these tasks to investigate your teen's one-hour after school detention for a minor discipline infraction? Probably not. The savvy parent keeps things like this in perspective.

Appealing a minor issue is going to make the principal think, "This parent appeals everything." The savvy parents wait to use their leverage for serious issues so they can say, "We have never appealed anything before now. We have always supported the school, but we feel this issue is really important. Can you help us?" Later in this chapter, we address more details on how to handle a serious discipline issue.

Now let's look at this same situation from a teacher's perspective.

For sake of argument, imagine that the issue in question places the teacher's word against your child's word. This situation is an age-old dilemma. Years ago the teacher's word always superseded that of the child (sometimes wrongly). If you appeal a minor discipline situation when the teacher says your teen did something and your child says that he or she didn't do it, what message are you sending to the teacher? By not appealing or making a big deal of a small issue you are showing the teacher a sign of good faith. You're telling that teacher I trust and support you. This support initially over a minor issue can pay dividends down the road later in the year. You can do some lasting harm to your relationship with school staff if you are not supportive in these situations.

It is important for your child to know that they must never be involved with "zero tolerance" violations, such as drugs, alcohol, weapons, and gang activities.

Insider's Note: No teen has ever had a life ruined by serving a detention.

MAJOR TROUBLE

We consider major trouble to be anything involving a suspension (either in or out of school) and, of course, expulsion. When a principal has to make this type of phone call to parents, they respond in all sorts of ways. Often, parents get emotional and have a hard time listening to the facts of the situation. If you get a call like this, our advice is to listen first before making any snap judgments. We have had parents tell us, "My kid didn't do it," before we could tell them what their child was accused of doing.

As you are listening, go into "fact-gathering" mode. Even though we recognize this is harder than it sounds, try to detach yourself from any emotions that arise. Between the moment you get the call from the principal and the point where you feel prepared to respond to the school, the information you need is: What is the school saying my teen has done? Is my teen guilty of this accusation? And, is the consequence appropriate?

As school principals, we can honestly say that the process can be overwhelming to parents. Sheepishly, we will also admit that many of our colleagues will treat the parent as the guilty ones rather than the child. Many parents get ashamed and question their own parenting skills. We are telling you loud and clear, "Get over it." This is not the time or place for these feelings of guilt. Amazing parents have kids who make stupid decisions. It happens; they're teenagers. They're going to mess up. It's what happens after the offense, and what your actions are, that make the difference.

This topic can be confusing and overwhelming so we will attempt to break it down as best we can. After each scenario, follow the steps outlined to help make the best of a bad situation.

Scenario A: My Kid Did It and We Accept the Consequences

Step 1 - Get all written documentation of the incident for your records.

Step 2 - Thank the administrator and have your teen write a letter of apology to the adult who wrote the discipline referral and copy the administrator who handled the discipline.

Step 3 - Always ask the administrator if your child can make up work missed if the consequence includes a suspension out of school. This is handled differently in every school division, so it is important to ask about it. Some school divisions make students do the work when suspended, and some school divisions do not allow work to be made up. (In other words, students often will be assigned zeros for each day that they are suspended.) If the administrator refuses, consider appealing this decision to the principal, especially if your teen previously has a solid record.

Step 4 - No matter what the answer is about make-up work from the school administration, you and your teen should nicely and respectfully contact the teacher about work that can be done to keep up. Some teachers might count the work for credit even though the school administration says, "No." At the very least, even if the work isn't counted for credit, your child's efforts will show the teacher how much he or she cares about the class and will help your teen stay "up to speed" when the suspension is over.

Scenario B: My Kid Did It, but I Think the Consequences Are Too Severe

Step 1 - Get all written documentation of the incident for your records.

Step 2 - Ask about the appeal process for your school division. This process should be outlined in the "Code of Conduct," and the administrator should be able to tell you about it. If the two versions don't match, follow the written, published procedure of the school division.

Step 3 - Specifically ask how many days you have before an appeal letter is due and to whom to direct your appeal letter.

Step 4 - Specifically ask if your teen can attend school during the appeal process. (Most likely, the answer will be yes, unless the principal deems your child and the infraction to be a safety issue or a major school disruption.) This step might be a consideration if your teen has a major test or assignment due the next day.

Step 5 - Before writing an appeal letter, research the "Code of Conduct" or discuss with the administrator if certain punishments are mandatory. For example, it might be a written policy to suspend a child three (3) days for being involved in a fight. So, if your teen was in a fight and got suspended three (3) days, it may not be worth appealing.

Step 6 - After the first five (5) steps, you can still decide to appeal the severity of the consequence in a clearly written letter of appeal to the correct person (usually directly to the school principal). See more on appeal letters later in this chapter.

Step 7 - If you accept that some of the original punishment is appropriate, have your teen serve that consequence during the appeal. For example, if your teen received a five-day suspension and you think a one-day suspension was appropriate, let your teen serve the one day of suspension.

Step 8 - After a decision is made, you must decide to accept it or appeal it to a higher authority. Consult the school's "Code of Conduct" to learn to whom you direct your next appeal letter and the time frame in which you need to deliver it. If you appeal it further, ask that person if your teen may attend school until a decision is made.

Step 9 - If all else fails and you really feel an injustice as been done, you can try to contact the school division's superintendent and your School Board representative. Only do either of these things after you have tried to follow the proper procedures and only do this if you feel there has been a major injustice done to your child.

Special note: Remember through all these interactions to remain professional and businesslike when dealing with school officials. Personal attacks, profanity, yelling, and screaming will only hurt your chances of a fair hearing.

Scenario C: I Believe My Kid Didn't Do It

Step 1 - Get all written documentation of the incident.

Step 2 - Request any other evidence the school has regarding your child's involvement in the incident, including witness statements, teacher statements, your own teen's statements, security video of any incident, or physical evidence. Keep in mind that the school may not be able to provide these things immediately as they will have to avoid any references to other students. Also, they are not allowed to provide you with other student or witness names when dealing with minors. Document your requests in writing (email is fine as written documentation) or with personal notations including date, time, and with whom you made the request.

Step 3 - If your teen identifies other potential witnesses who can verify their version of the incident, provide these names to the school administration and request that they be interviewed and that you be provided a summary of the discussion.

Step 4 - Ask about the appeal process for your school division. The process should be outlined in the "Code of Conduct," and the administrator should be able to tell you about it. If the two versions don't match, follow the written, published procedure of the school division.

Step 5 - Specifically ask how many days you have to write an appeal letter and to whom you should direct your appeal letter.

Step 6 - Specifically ask if your teen can attend school during the appeal process. (This will most likely be granted unless the principal deems your teen and the infraction to be a safety issue or a major school disruption.) Your child's attendance might be a consideration if your teen has a major test or assignment due the next day.

Step 7 - Have a serious discussion with your child. Make sure that your teen understands that you will defend them, but you want the truth now. Your teen needs to understand you are putting your reputation on the line.

Step 8 - After the first seven (7) steps, you may still decide to appeal the school decision regarding the incident by writing a clearly stated letter of appeal to the correct person (usually directly to the school principal). See more on appeal letters later in this chapter.

Step 9 - After a decision is made by the school principal, you must decide to accept it or appeal it to a higher authority. Consult the school's "Code of Conduct" to learn to whom you direct your next appeal letter and the time frame in which you need to deliver it. If you appeal it to a higher level, ask that person if your teen may attend school until a decision is made.

Step 10 - If all else fails and you really feel an injustice has been done, you can try to contact the school division's superintendent and your School Board representative. Only do either of these things after you have tried to follow the proper procedures and only do this if you feel it is a major injustice to your child.

Special note: Remember through all of this to remain professional and businesslike when dealing with school officials. Personal attacks, profanity, yelling, and screaming will only hurt your chances of a fair hearing.

Scenario D: My Kid Really Messed Up and the School Is Talking About Expulsion

Step 1 - Get all written documentation of the incident.

Step 2 - Request any other evidence the school has regarding your teen's involvement with the incident, including witness statements, teacher statements, your own teen's statements, security video of any incident, or physical evidence. Keep in mind that the school may not be able to provide these things immediately as they will have to avoid any references to other students. They are not allowed to provide you with other student or witness names when dealing with minors.

Step 3 - Read very carefully your school division's "Code of Conduct" regarding expulsion proceedings. Become an expert in these procedures. These procedures will contain the due process to be followed to protect the rights of your teen. You and your child will be afforded some sort of meetings/hearings with the school principal; as well as a hearing officer and possibly the School Board.

Step 4 - Decide which line of defense you are going to take. Either the "my child is innocent" approach or the "ask for mercy from the court" approach will determine your course of action.

Step 5 - Begin to take actions to put you and your teen in a good position for any hearings held. Actions such as: (a) request character reference letters from other adults such as friends, bosses, church/synagogue leaders, coaches, etc. In fact, many savvy parents seen in these situations ask their child's current teachers for a recommendation letter and (b) take appropriate actions at home. In other words, if you are asked by a school official what you have done as a parent to discipline your teen, how would you answer? To indicate that you are taking your teen's actions seriously, consider enforcing some at home discipline before any administrative hearing. Here are some actions we have seen to be effective in the past:

- Place your teen on restriction (no social interactions).
- Take away video games, cell phones, iPods, Internet access.
- Make sure your child keeps up with school work (see note after step 9 regarding this issue).
- Don't allow contact with friends.
- Give extra chores at home.
- Consider other actions:
  - Counseling.
  - Drug testing (if appropriate).
  - Anger management counseling (if appropriate).
  - Meet with church/synagogue leader.

Step 6 - During each and every hearing treat the school officials with respect in a professional manner. Acting rude, disrespectful, and condescending will only negatively impact your child and the situation. It seems silly to have to write these words, but make sure you and your teen attend any hearing well dressed and properly groomed. While we completely understand that some folks don't have the most expensive clothes, the reality is that we have seen people come in without showering, without shaving, in torn and tattered clothing, and even clothing that had not been washed in what appeared to be a very long time.

Step 7 - In some cases, expulsion is required by state law for certain offenses unless you can provide extraordinary reasons for an exception. Make sure to articulate what makes your teen different, why your child is not a safety threat to the school and other students, and any other mitigating factors that may have led to his or her behavior (traumatic episodes in teen's life, medications, family fight the night before, etc.). Unfortunately, saying that "My child a good kid," isn't enough here as every serious case we have dealt with as principals, the parents always say, "My child is a good kid."

Step 8 - Prepare your teen to be respectful and not lose his or her temper. Whoever is conducting the hearing wants to know that your teen can handle the pressure. In fact, frequently, hearing officers and school lawyers will purposefully try to rattle the student to further demonstrate justification for expelling the child. Your teen needs to remain composed, speak clearly, have a goal for education and the future, be remorseful, understand the seriousness of the situation and, most importantly, be extremely respectful of all adults involved.

Step 9 - Keep appealing as high as you can based on the procedures of your school division. Be aware that technically, when you appeal, the punishment could actually be increased, but we've seen it happen only rarely. What usually happens at every level of appeal is that the consequence gets softened a bit based on the genuineness and quality of your appeal.

Step 10 - If or when you reach the School Board level, they will be interested in your control of the situation. This may be your entire school board or just a "committee" of the school board. School Boards love parents who have enacted serious consequences at home and have taken the charges against the student seriously. This fact is important whether or not you agree with the school's accusations. If, as a parent, you take a relaxed approach to this situation, it will severely hamper your credibility. School Boards are much more likely to modify the consequences in your favor if they are assured that your teen has learned a lesson, is safe to be back in school, and will never do these things again. Please note that actions speak volumes compared to words in this situation. Simply saying that your teen is a good kid and that this will never happen again will not suffice. You must show the School Board the actions you have taken and are planning to take to help your child recover from this issue.

Special note: When dealing with School Board members it is of the utmost importance to treat them with respect. Even if you are angry with the school and the principal, do not direct this anger at the School Board. This will hurt your teen's case. When it reaches their level, the School Board members, with the consultation of their lawyer, make the decision. Treat them with respect and realize you need them to sympathize and understand your dilemma and connect with you as a parent who needs their help.

Expulsion can mean a lot of different things. It can mean a 365-day expulsion, or it can be for a shorter period of time. Some school divisions will provide some level of service, but some school divisions will provide no service at all (unless your child is in Special Education and then, by law, your child must be provided some level of service). One note on appealing to a higher authority: Go as high as you can go. However, if you are offered a "deal" at a lower level, strongly consider accepting it. In some cases, a School Board will respond negatively if you turned down a chance for a lightened sentence earlier in the procedure.

NOTES ON EXPULSION PROCEEDINGS

When the school begins to talk about expulsion, you need to be on high alert. Expulsion in schools is tantamount to the death penalty in criminal proceedings. What the school is talking about is taking away all educational services for a period of time. If you are ever in this situation, you need to consider the following questions:

What Happens with Schoolwork During These Proceedings?

When a student is being considered for expulsion, the process can take weeks and sometimes even months. Usually, a student will be suspended out of school for five to ten days. During the first ten days of suspension, the school division is not required to provide any instruction to your child. Remember, this requirement does not stop you from contacting the teachers and requesting school work. This action will help your teen stay busy and current with the work in classes, and it always looks good to School Board members when a student takes this type of initiative. If the settlement of the problem takes more than ten school days, the school division should provide some basic level of service from day eleven until the matter is fully resolved. This basic level of service can be as little as having a staff member deliver work to be completed from teachers. Whatever educational opportunity is offered to you, please take advantage of it. If you refuse any educational service, you are sending a clear message that you have given up, your teen has given up, and that you are not grateful for what is being provided.

Is My Child Receiving Due Process?

Another aspect of all disciplinary infractions is due process. Every student is entitled to some level of Due Process. The level of Due Process is connected to the severity of the punishment. In other words, if your child gets a referral for skipping a class and the consequence is a Saturday detention, Due Process can be satisfied at a basic level. This level usually means that students are given an opportunity to hear the "charges" against them (in this case the date and class they skipped) and are given an opportunity to give their side of the story.

As the severity of the consequence rises to suspension and expulsion, students are entitled to more Due Process to protect their rights. For example, often times before a principal can make a recommendation for expulsion there must be some sort of conference or hearing with the child and parent. At the conference the child and parent hear the formal charges, can present their witnesses, give their side of the story, etc.

If you feel your teen has not been afforded with the proper Due Process, you might contact a lawyer (one that knows educational law well).

WRITING AN APPEAL LETTER

When you write an appeal letter, include the following three elements. One, the letter must contain your child's name and a description of the incident as you understand it. Two, it must contain exactly what and why you are appealing. Three, it is wise to include a suggestion on how you would see this matter resolved. We recommend that you also include any steps you are taking to help remediate your child's behavior.

An appeal letter should be written logically and without emotion. Refrain from personal attacks against the school principal, a teacher, or any other staff member. Many times, parents will write these letters quickly without thinking through the issue; therefore, the letter come across as a "rant" rather than a formal, serious appeal. We have seen parents who simply write that they want to appeal the consequence given but don't explain why. In their mind, an injustice was done. In other words, they don't explain the basis for their appeal. Many parents do not clearly state the purpose of their appeal letter. If you are okay with your teen serving a day of out-of-school suspension, but would like him or her to be able to make up work for credit, be clear about this request. Specifically include your idea for an appropriate consequence.

> *Insider's Note: It is important for parents to know what disciplinary infractions stay in a child's permanent record. In some school districts, all discipline gets expunged at the end of the school year. In other school districts, only suspension days stay in the record. In some districts, all discipline referrals stay in the permanent record. Make sure to ask about this policy when you begin the process. An understanding of what remains in your teen's discipline record will put perspective on the whole situation.*

It is important that you know what you can actually appeal. For example, a solution principals may use is to make an agreement about future issues with the teen. For example, the consequence may be lessened if the student and parent agree to a discipline contract, a probationary period, if you will. Sometimes parents will be worried about their child's permanent record. A compromise is an agreement to remove an infraction from the record if the teen has no further infractions.

Appeal letters are the place you want to point out procedural mistakes you believe have been made when dealing with your child's situation. Again, consult your school division's Code of Conduct or your school's handbook, which should outline the normal procedures for disciplinary infractions. For example, if the school handbook states that a student gets a one hour after school detention for skipping class, but your teen was assigned a one day of out-of-school suspension, this would be a procedural mistake since the school did not follow its own policy. As mentioned above in the due process section, if you teen did not receive a chance to explain his or her side of the story, than that procedural mistake should be pointed out in the letter of appeal.

Many times when experienced principals recognize that their staff may have not handled the situation appropriately, they will look for a compromise with the parent. In other words, they don't want to excuse a student's guilt, but they do recognize the fact that the school could have handled the situation better.

One special note about any appeal or agreement made with the school principal or any school official. Do not be afraid to ask for a response from your appeal in writing, including any special agreements. Ask that any documentation from the appeal be placed in your student's discipline file as a matter of record. To ensure consistency, you need to have documentation to help in these types of circumstances. Remember if it's not in writing, you are taking a big risk.

Finally, if your school division has a policy in place that states certain consequences cannot be appealed above the principal, our experience is that you should not be deterred from going above the principal. Sometimes, it may be true and you may get turned down from the higher authority. If that happens, it is no big deal. Often times, however, the principal's supervisor will review your child's situation and possibly offer you some relief. Only consider going over the principal's head in cases of out-of-school suspension. Lesser consequences should not be appealed above the principal.

HIRING A LAWYER

Some parents ask if they should hire a lawyer when they find them-selves involved in a major disciplinary issue with their teen. For this tough question, we wish we could give you a definitive answer. Let us begin by reiterating that we are high school principals and are not in the business of giving out legal advice. That being said, because of our jobs we have had many experiences that involved parents bringing attorneys into disciplinary proceedings. In these situations, our experiences have been mixed. We have seen some really poor lawyers make things worse for the very students they represent. On the other hand, there have been a few cases where having a lawyer present might have had a positive impact on the outcome of the student's case.

In our personal experience, a respectful, honest, genuine student speaking from the heart, apologizing and asking for mercy works, just as well, if not better, than a high-priced lawyer. It is important to understand, however, that neither approach is likely to get you out of trouble completely. What we are saying is that, in our experience, having a lawyer rarely makes a substantial difference (either good or bad) in the outcome of a disciplinary hearing.

In our experience, we have seen two exceptions where having legal representation can make a difference. The first is when the parents of the student in trouble were unable control their child's statements, attitude, and/or temper. In this situation, a skilled lawyer is often able to assist with this task. The second exception is when the family decides to fight what they believe is an infringement upon a student's constitutional rights (usually freedom of speech or religion). In these cases, a savvy lawyer can really make a difference.

If you do decide to hire a lawyer, make sure to get one with experience in educational law. This experience can make a big difference, as the School Board's attorney will be an expert in educational law and will make an unprepared lawyer or one unfamiliar with educational law look inadequate.

Chapter Twelve

A Brief Look Forward

As you approach the end of your teen's freshman year, you have a great deal to celebrate. With our advice, you will hopefully have had a relatively easy year, and you've witnessed your teen make a smooth transition to high school. Now you are ready to help your child tackle the next segment of their high school career: the sophomore year.

Sophomore, literally translated from Greek, means "wise fool." This grade level did not receive this moniker by chance. Tenth-graders have a year of high school under their belts, and this, in their minds, makes them an expert in all things high school. They believe they have it all figured out. They know the score. Unfortunately, they are still beginners and are often prone to making really, really bad decisions.

> *Insider's Tip: Beware of the "sophomore slump". If your sophomore is going to really mess up, it will be in the first few weeks of sophomore year. If you can keep them on track during this crucial period, chances are they will keep it together all year. Spend those first few weeks reinforcing the good habits that got them through their freshman year.*

Being the parent of a sophomore, however, is generally much easier than being the parent of a freshman. Sophomores generally have all the tools they need to experience success. All they need is your help remembering how to use those tools and why they were important in their last year's success.

THE GOOD NEWS: ACHIEVING ACADEMIC SUCCESS AS A SOPHOMORE

Chances are that your freshman recognized there was a significant

Andres Rodriguez

It may seem a lifetime away, but you will be celebrating your teen's graduation from high school before you know it.

increase in the caliber of academic work expected in their ninth grade classes. This recognition is normal. There is generally a noticeable increase in both the amount and depth of the scholarship required of ninth graders. Here is some good news: In general, the academic expectations in tenth grade are similar to those expected in ninth grade. You don't generally see a great deal of difference in the workload or the depth of thought expected of students between English 9 and English 10, for instance. Earth Science and Biology are also generally regarded as introductory lab sciences so they generally expect similar academic production. The same thing goes for Algebra I and Geometry. Therefore, if your teen was academically successful in the ninth grade year, you can generally assume that equally good success will be enjoyed (or even better, since they have grown and matured one year) in their sophomore year.

Our advice to you as parents of sophomores is to re-establish your academic protocols and procedures with your teen. This attitude doesn't mean that these "rules" have to be the same as they were in the freshman year, but again, we suggest that you don't want your newly minted sophomore to think that now they are "on their own." They still need to know that you are interested and engaged in their academic well-being. Sit down with your rising sophomore in the weeks before the beginning of the school year and discuss what these academic protocols and procedures might be. Let your teen have more input. Discuss what went well last year, which of the protocols might be good to keep, and which of them might you be ready to decrease. This is a good time to allow your teen to begin to experiment with more independency in their work. Establish a clear understanding that this is a trial period, however, and if you determine that your teen is slipping, you may want to reintegrate some of the protocols that worked in the freshman year back into the routine.

MORE GOOD NEWS: THE SOCIAL LIFE OF SOPHOMORES

Sophomores are hilarious. As high school insiders, it is amazing to watch this group come back to school at the beginning of their tenth grade year. We see students who were trying so hard to be mature and grown up last year (as freshmen) come back as if they regressed a full two years in maturity over the summer. They no longer have the anxiety and nerves they had as freshmen; they are no longer trying to impress anyone; they know that they are not "upperclassmen" yet. Therefore, it's almost as if they have come to terms with their position in the school and decided, "To heck with it. Let's just be ourselves." And they are goofy and fun!

Further good news is that generally, by the end of the freshman year, sophomores have established who they are and who they are going to hang out with, so as parents, you are not going to be dealing with having to monitor new sets of friends every month.

THE BAD NEWS: "WHERE DID THIS ATTITUDE COME FROM?"

Unfortunately, you may notice a different attitude from your sophomore than you noticed in his or her ninth grade year. Sophomores seem to develop the impression that they know how to succeed on their own and no longer need much guidance for their parents. We have had hundreds of parents of sophomores in our offices asking us why their teen keeps telling them to "Shut up!" and informing them that "They don't know anything." We usually smile, inform them that this is very normal, and advise them to wait until sometime in the second month of their teen's junior year, when all of a sudden, most students realize that they still need a great deal of help and support from their parents. Our best words of advice to parents on this issue are to tell them to relax and then we say, "This too shall pass."

In general, if your student has been able to stay on track during the freshman year, the odds are that they will continue to experience that same success during their sophomore year.

Final Thoughts

After sharing this book with our friends, family members, colleagues, and members of our school communities, the response we received was nearly always the same. They would exclaim, "Oh my word! How does anyone ever survive high school?" And upon reflection, we understand the shock people feel when they hear us relate the scary and intimidating issues that face high school aged students and their parents during high school. This crucial time period truly is fraught with potential hazards and pitfalls for a teen.

Yet, despite these challenges, we can say without any reservations: We love high school! Every year we witness countless numbers of students successfully navigate their high school experience. They have fun; they develop lifelong friends; and form lifelong memories. They gain incredible amounts of knowledge, have opportunities to develop, practice, and master skills they will rely upon as they move forward into their post-secondary lives, whether that is in the workplace or in college or university. We see students involved in music groups, theater troupes, athletic teams, and curricular clubs, just to name a few of the myriad of activities students enjoy every day of their high school careers. We see, in short, young teenagers developing into the educated, able, and engaged citizenry of our great country. High school is a great place to be!

We hope that the lessons we have shared in this book make the transition of your ninth-grade student to high school a smoother, more successful, and even a more enjoyable experience for both your student and yourself. We further hope that the advice we've offered puts your teen on the path to not only survive, but also thrive during this crucial first year of high school. Finally, we hope the habits and systems that we have helped you develop with your teen will continue to foster success throughout their high school career.

Appendix A

Insider's Guide Sample Forms

Parent(s)	Rising Ninth Grade Student
What are your dreams for the future for your teen? (Reach for the stars!) There is no question that the kid is a natural at baseball– I think he has a chance to make it to the majors! This is both of our dreams, really. I want to support him in this as much as possible.	*What are your dreams for the future? (Reach for the stars!)* I will be a professional baseball player – a power hitting first baseman. I will be drafted out of high school and will be in the major leagues within 3 years of graduating from high school. I'm going to be rich and famous!
What will it take for your teen to achieve these dreams? We both know that this is a long shot – in order for him to go all the way he will have to be literally one in a million. Practice and practice and practice. Play year-round with a commitment that can't be questioned. Excellence on the field at all times. But he can do it!	*What will it take for you to achieve these dreams?* I will have to be among the very best ball players in the country. I need to have a incredible freshman year both in school ball and in travel ball to get the attention of the scouts. I will also have to really commit to lifting weights and getting stronger and faster – train, train, train.
What is a great "back-up plan" for your teen? I know all he thinks about is baseball . . . but this will change. I think a great back up plan would be to go to a four year college to study business administration	*What is your "back-up plan" for your future?* I will get a baseball scholarship and study to become a teacher. I really appreciate Mr. Banks and all he has done for me as my baseball coach. If I can't be a major league player, I want to be a coach so I can help others learn the game that I love.
What will it take for your teen to achieve this "back-up plan"? Good grades and solid academic focus. Keep his nose clean and make sure he is an attractive candidate for college admissions.	*What will it take to achieve this "back-up plan"?* A good high school baseball career at high school and good enough grades not to scare the college coaches away so I can get the free ride to go to college.

Sample Insider's Edge Vision Inventory 1

Parent(s)	*Rising Ninth Grade Student*
What are your dreams for the future for your teen? (Reach for the stars!) I would like for my teenager to graduate high school and go to a four-year university. I want my child to be happy and have it a little better than I have had it.	*What are your dreams for the future? (Reach for the stars!)* Graduate. Go to college. Get a good job and enjoy life. Hang out with my friends.
What will it take for your teen to achieve these dreams? Take some advanced/college-prep. classes. Prepare for and take the SAT or ACT test. Do homework, study for tests, stay out of trouble. Get involved in some extracurricular clubs or activities.	*What will it take for you to achieve these dreams?* Study and pass my classes.
What is a great "back-up plan" for your teen? Go to the community college for 2 years and then transfer to a university.	*What is your "back-up plan" for your future?* Go to the community college for 2 years and then transfer to a university. Get a good job and enjoy life. Hang out with my friends.
What will it take for your teen to achieve this "back-up plan"? Graduate high school. Do homework, study for tests, stay out of trouble. Get a job to help pay for college.	*What will it take to achieve this "back-up plan"?* Graduate high school by studying and passing my classes. Do well at the community college.

Sample Insider's Edge Vision Inventory 2

POST-SECONDARY PLAN	
Primary Ambitions	*Realistic "Back-Up" Plan*
State your chosen plan: Admission to an Ivy league school, preferably Harvard or Yale.	*State your chosen back-up plan:* Admission to a top state school with an academic scholarship.
What level of education, training, preparation, and other factors will you need to achieve this goal? *Education:* I will have to complete the most rigorous and challenging academic course of study available at the high school. *Training:* I will have to also have another skill or aptitude to make me stand out from the rest – maybe become a certified EMT and work on the Rescue Squad. *Preparation:* I should enroll in SAT classes to ensure that I score at the very top when compared to the rest of my grade at the national level. *Other factors:* I need to be ranked #1 in my class to be considered for these schools.	*What level of education, training, preparation, and other factors will you need to achieve this goal?* *Education:* I will have to take academically rigorous classes, especially the AP classes in my junior and senior year. *Training:* I should have some other type of extra-curricular leadership position to flesh out my resume. *Preparation:* I should make sure that I am in position to score well on SATs and other tests to show that I am a good candidate for college success. *Other factors:* I should make sure that I stay in the top 15% of the class, and, if possible, hold a leadership positions.
Describe what type of high school achievement will likely be necessary for you to realize this ambition: Straight A's all four years, as many AP classes as possible to "pump up" the GPA, no negative issues whatsoever.	*Describe what type of high school achievement will likely be necessary for you to realize this ambition:* All A's and B's during high school. A good number of AP classes to show the college that I am a serious student.
What other activities will increase your chances of realizing this goal? Leadership positions, something really special – publish a work?	*What other activities will increase your chances of realizing this goal?* Involvement in extra-curricular activities that will show I am "well-rounded".

Sample Insider's Edge Post-Secondary Plan

Appendix B

Resources for Parents of High School Students

Many of the parents who we work with on a daily basis requested that we gather together some of the great online resources available to students and parents. Many of these resources are completely free. Visit these sites to see what they can do for you.

ACADEMIC RESOURCES

Literacy Matters
Literacy Matters is one of the world's leading nonprofit education organizations promoting literacy and institutional reform. Currently, the project is funded by the Annenberg Foundation and the U.S. Department of Education.
www.literacymatters.org/parents/ideas.htm

NCTE: The National Council of Teachers of English
NCTE is a professional organization for educators. Their website offers up-to-date information and news for parents, as well as tips for parent involvement.
www.ncte.org/parents

Parent Academic Resources Incorporated
This insightful and informative site aims to empower parents during their children's adolescent years, increase parent involvement, and ultimately foster high levels of student learning.
www.academicresources.org/learning.html

PBS *It's My Life*
It's My Life is funded by the Corporation for Public Broadcasting to create safe educational online media activities for teenagers. Parents and children can read informative articles, share stories, play games, and get advice from experts.
pbskids.org/itsmylife/parents/resources/highschool.html

ProofWriter™— The Online Writing Tool
New service for students provides quick analysis of written documents along with helpful grammar, usage, mechanics and style rules designed to increase learning and encourage better writing skills.
www.proofwriter.ets.org

Scholarly Societies Project
Provides access to information about scholarly societies across the world.
www.scholarly-societies.org/

RESOURCES FOR POSTECONDARY PLANNING

Nelnet
This site provides information for planning and financing education along with planning careers.
www.nelnet.com

Office of Postsecondary Education
This site provides information for students preparing for their future.
www.ed.gov/students/prep/college/index.html

Mapping Your Future
This site provides students and parents with information on financial strategies, career options, and college planning.
www.mappingyourfuture.org

PREPARATION FOR COLLEGE ENTRANCE EXAMINATIONS

ACT
This site provides information about registering for the ACT test; and provides students practice tests to prepare for the ACT examination.
www.act.org

The College Board
This site provides information about registering for the SAT test, and provides help to students who want to prepare for the SAT. www.collegeboard.com

Educational Testing Service
Provides practice tests and resources for parents and students who are interested in Advanced Placement (AP), PSAT, and other educational tests. www.ets.org

COLLEGE SEARCH INFORMATION

College Opportunities OnLine (COOL)
This site allows prospective students to see and compare profiles of colleges and universities across the nation. www.nces.ed.gov/collegenavigator

College Portrait
This site provides accountability data on institutional performance and is sponsored by the National Association of State Universities and Land-Grant Colleges and by the American Association of State Colleges and Universities. www.collegeportraits.org

College.gov
This site is designed by students and sponsored by the U.S. Department of Education. www.college.gov/wps/portal

CollegeNET
This site provides links for college searches, applications, and scholarships. www.cnsearch.collegenet.com/cgi-bin/CN/index

FastWeb
Registration is required for this site; it provides searches for colleges, scholarships, jobs, and internships.
www.fastweb.com

GoCollege
This site provides resources for admissions, education options, college survival, and financial aid.
www.gocollege.com

Thompson Peterson's
This site provides search tools for colleges and universities, articles, and resources to help find the right school.
www.petersons.com

RESOURCES ABOUT PAYING FOR COLLEGE AND FINANCIAL AID

"Cash for College" Program - N.A.S.F.A.A.
This site provides information on paying for college and applying for financial aid.
www.nasfaa.org/subhomes/cash4college/index2.html

College Answer
This site from Sallie Mae offers college planning tools in both English and Spanish.
www.collegeanswer.com/index.jsp

College Is Possible
A service offered by the American Council on Education, this site provides parents and students resources for paying, preparing, and choosing the right college.
www.acenet.edu/AM/Template.cfm?Section=CIP1

Federal Student Financial Assistance
This site provides information on preparing for and funding education beyond high school.
www.studentaid.ed.gov/PORTALSWebApp/students/english/index.jsp

Fund Finder (by The College Board)
This site provides information on how to save or pay for college and financial aid basics.
www.collegeboard.com/student/pay/add-it-up/index.html

Free Application for Federal Student Aid (FAFSA)
This site show students and parents to how fill out the FAFSA with step-by-step instructions.
www.fafsa.ed.gov

Free Scholarship Search
This site provides links to more than 40 free online scholarship search sites.
www.college-scholarships.com/free_scholarship_searches.htm

National Student Loan Data System (NSLDS)
This site allows you to check your student loan records; you will need your FAFSA PIN to access your NSLDS records.
www.nslds.ed.gov/nslds_SA

Scholarship Experts
This site requires registration and provides free scholarship searches.
www.scholarshipexperts.com

Scholarships.com
This site provides links for scholarship searches; college searches; and scholarship providers.
www.scholarships.com

The SmartStudent Guide to Financial Aid
This site provides information on scholarships, loans, military aid, and saving for college.
www.finaid.org

RESOURCES FOR PARENTS OF STUDENTS WITH DISABILITIES

DisabilityInfo.gov
This site offers good information on education programs and resources through the federal government for those who are disabled.
www.disability.gov/education

GENERAL EDUCATION RESOURCES

The College Board – Advanced Placement Program ®
This site provides information and answers to frequently asked questions about the Advanced Placement (AP) program.
www.collegeboard.com/student/testing/ap/about.html

International Baccalaureate ® Programme (IB)
This site provides information and answers to frequently asked questions about the IB program.
www.ibo.org

NEA National Education Association
The National Education Association is a volunteer-based organization committed to advancing the cause of public education.
www.nea.org/parents/index.html

Students.gov
Provides students and parents with easy to access information and resources from the U.S. government regarding higher education.
www.students.gov/STUGOVWebApp/Public

U.S. Department of Education

This site provides questions and answers for students, parents, teachers, and administrators.
www.ed.gov/students/landing.jhtml?src=pn

Index

19.95   7/12/10